SIN AND PENANCE

SIN AND PENANCE

Insights Into the Mystery of Salvation

REV. PETER RIGA

St. John Vianney Seminary, Buffalo, New York

THE BRUCE PUBLISHING COMPANY

MILWAUKEE

NIHIL OBSTAT:

Nelson W. Logal
Censor deputatus

IMPRIMATUR:

✠ Josephus Aloisius Burke
Episcopus Buffalensis
Die 30ª Novembris, 1961

The nihil obstat and imprimatur are official declarations that
a book or pamphlet is free of doctrinal or moral error. No
implication is contained therein that those who have granted
the nihil obstat and imprimatur agree with the contents,
opinions, or statements expressed.

Library of Congress Catalog Card Number: 62–19191

For Marie Claire

. . . *Sicut Christus Ecclesiam.*

— Eph 5:25

Contents

Introduction

I

The mystery of sin is the story of salvation, for the destruction of sin was, as St. Paul reminds us, a fundamental reason for the Incarnation. "By sending his Son in a nature like that of sinful man and in order to remove sin, he had condemned sin by the incarnation" (Rom 8:3).*

To bring about the destruction of sin, God became man and lived and died in the nature of a mortal human being. He "emptied himself by taking the nature of a slave, fashioned as he was to the likeness of men and recognized by outward appearance as man" (Phil 2:7). The power of His divinity was purposely hidden beneath the veil of His sacred humanity. The whole theme of St. John's Gospel was to reveal this divinity, which had become incarnate, to men whose eyes had to become the eyes of faith. "And the Word became man and lived among us; and we have looked upon his glory — such a glory as befits the Father's only-begotten Son" (Jn 1:14). The great drama of the Fourth Gospel portrays for us the struggle of evil, the Kingdom of Satan, personified in the unbelief of the Jews despite the many signs worked before their very eyes, vs. the Light, the Kingdom of God, which was equated with those who believed and followed Christ.[1] "The light has come into the world, but men loved the darkness more than the light, because their lives were bad. Only an evildoer hates the light and refuses

---

* Throughout the book, texts of the New Testament are taken from the Kleist-Lilly translation (Milwaukee, 1954). Texts of the Old Testament are from the new Confraternity translation from the original languages (Paterson, N. J., 1961).

[1] I. De la Potterie, "Le Péché, c'est l'Iniquité," Nou. Rev. Théo., 78 (Sept.–Oct., 1956), 785–788.

to face the light, for fear his practices may be exposed; but one who lives up to the truth faces the light, so that everyone can see that his life is lived in union with God" (Jn 3:19–21). Thus the light in the world is the Incarnate Word who has come to reveal the Father and the way to the Father. Refusal to believe in the Incarnate Word is the primary sin; to accept Him is to accept truth and light. Christ became and still is "the sign of contradiction for the rise and fall of many in Israel" (Lk 2:34). The crucified Christ, who was delivered up because of sin, becomes "to the Jews certainly a stumbling block and to the Gentiles an absurdity" (1 Cor 1:23). And almost with a cry of gladness and joy, St. Paul proclaims: "The Jews demand miracles and the Greeks look for 'wisdom,' but we, for our part, preach a crucified Christ . . ." who is "the power of God and the wisdom of God" (*ibid.*).

Thus the two themes of St. John and St. Paul are happily united in one Christology: by His humiliation, by and through His weak humanity, the power of God's glory and salvation makes itself accessible to men. Men must come to recognize that God's power of salvation is a crucified son of a carpenter of Nazareth.[2] That is the way of God with men; he "chose what the world holds foolish, to put to shame the wise, and what the world holds weak God chose to put to shame the mighty . . ." (1 Cor 1:27). God has willed that men come to Him through His incarnate, crucified, and risen Son. "Of course, no one has ever ascended into heaven but there is one who has come down from heaven, the Son of Man, whose home was in heaven. And just as Moses lifted up the serpent in the desert, so the Son of Man must needs be lifted up, that everyone who believes in him may have eternal life" (Jn 3:13–14). Anyone who has

---

[2] "The gospel is God's word, and His power radiating through human shortcomings. It is symbolized by the cross of Christ. Christianity is founded precisely upon that which, in the eyes of men, is merely weak and shameful — the cross. The power of God works upon precisely that." L. Cerfaux, *Christ in the Theology of St. Paul* (New York, 1959), p. 156; see also H. Schillerbuck, *Die Sacramentale Heilseconomie* (Antwerpen, 1952), pp. 125–183; French translation, *Le Christ: Sacrement de la Rencontre de Dieu* (Paris, 1960).

studied the meaning of the "Son of Man" in the Gospel of John knows that the evangelist sums up the whole of Christ's salvific mission in that one phrase, which can just as easily be transcribed as Christ who was born, lived, died, and rose from the tomb.[3] Christ is the incarnate revelation of the Father, and for that very reason He is "scandal for the Jews and an absurdity for the Gentiles."

That Christ would be a scandal is understandable enough. At least the first Christians were very conscious of this in the elaboration of their theology of the crucifixion and death of Christ.[4] But even more scandalous is that Christ left all His salvific powers in the hands of His bride, the Church. In her, God makes Himself continually visible to the eyes of the faithful, and, in the words of Bossuet, "she is Christ spread abroad and communicated." In other words, just as Christ used His sacred and visible humanity to manifest the divinity and the salvific power of God, so now, after His Ascension into heaven, He has willed to communicate these salvific powers to His visible mystical body which is the Church.[5] The body of Christ manifests the spiritual activity of the Christ who has been raised on high in glory; the Church, identified with this glorious body, is the realization of this same activity. In the words of Msgr. Cerfaux: "How are we to express the due relation of the Body of Christ which is the Church, to the physical body which belonged to Christ as a person? They must be identified in a mystical way. The glorified body of Christ is the dwelling place of the fullness of the Godhead. Being identified with this body, the Church in its turn receives the fullness of divine life. As the glorified body of Christ is the full flowering of His person, so also is the Church."[6] Thus all the sanctifying powers of Christ have been

---

[3] Ch. Dodd, *The Interpretation of the Fourth Gospel* (Cambridge, 1955), pp. 244–249; Fr. Lagrange, *Evangile Selon Saint Jean* (Paris, 1947), p. 25; R. Bultmann and A. Weiser, *Faith* (London, 1961), pp. 97–110.

[4] P. Benoit, "La Loi de la Croix," *Exégèse et Théologie*, II (Paris, 1961), pp. 29–37.

[5] L. Cerfaux, *The Church in the Theology of St. Paul* (New York, 1959), p. 325. Y. Congar, *Christ, Our Lady and the Church* (New York, 1956), pp. 54–68. [6] L. Cerfaux, op. cit., p. 343.

communicated to His mystical and visible body which is the Church. In this visible temple alone can salvation be found and from her alone pour out the waters of salvation.[7] "Such language is hard to bear; who can listen to it!" (Jn 6:60.) The Jews of old were scandalized by the presence and the words of Christ. If we no longer experience the shock of this reality, is the reason perhaps that our faith has lost its cutting edge? "Yet if all this is so, there is something yet more 'scandalous' and 'foolish' about belief in the Church where the divine is not only united with the human, but presents itself to us by way of the all-too-human, and that without any alternative."[8] In spite of the fact that she is the body of Christ, still the Church's members, lay and clerical, are not the inheritors of the privilege which caused Christ to say: "Which of you shall convince me of sin?" The Church is more a paradox than Christ and presents mankind with an even greater contrast. If a purification and transformation of vision is necessary to look on Christ without being scandalized, how much more is it necessary when we look on the Church?[9] And yet it is by her and through her and in her alone that we attain Christ. Her radiance and visibility are those of Christ and outside of her there is absolutely no salvation. This should not come as too great a shock to us. God continuously chose and chooses what is weak to bring about His designs: the Jews of old; the humanity of Christ; the fragility of the Church; the simple elements of the sacraments. But in each case, beneath the weak veils, there and there alone is the power and salvation of God.

---

[7] It is not necessary to cite the many Patristic passages in this regard. It is sufficient to quote the great Western doctor, St. Augustine: "Whence the Catholic Church is alone the body of Christ. . . . Outside this body the Holy Spirit gives life to no one. . . . For those who are outside the Church do not have the Holy Spirit." *In Joann.*, Tract. XXVII, no. II (P.L., 35, 1621).

[8] H. De Lubac, *The Splendour of the Church* (New York, 1956), p. 27. For contrast in the Protestant conception, see R. M. Brown, *The Spirit of Protestantism* (New York, 1961).

[9] C. Journet, *The Church of the Word Incarnate*, I (New York, 1954), pp. XXVII–XXVIII. Yet it must be noted with Msgr. Journet that "the sins of her members are not to be identified with the Church, or the imperfections of Christians with Christianity. It is not these that constitute her, or make her visible. . . ."

II

What has all this to do with the sacrament of penance? Everything, for the seven sacraments are nothing more than the concrete extension and application of divine power in the Church.[10] The sacraments are the means of salvation, and they are so only because they are extensions of the unique means of salvation which is the Church. Each of the sacraments incorporates a person into the Church, or unites him more deeply to the Church and thus to Christ. By baptism, the Christian is incorporated into the Church, and by and through that very fact he becomes a true "member of Christ." In baptism, the Christian has died to sin and has risen with Christ: "Do you not know that all of us who have been baptized into union with Christ Jesus have been buried in death with him by means of Baptism, in order that, just as Christ was raised from the dead by the glorious power of the Father, so we also may conduct ourselves by a new principle of life?" (Rom 6:3–5.) Dead to sin and incorporated into the Church, the Christian lives the very life of Christ. In such a context and following such a course, the Christian is incapable of sin. "No one who is a child of God sins, because the life-germ implanted by God abides in him, and so, he cannot sin" (1 Jn 3:9); that is, those who follow the logic and the consequence of their baptism are radically incapable of sin.[11]

But the course of history has proved far different. Christians, even after baptism, returned to all their former sins. How were they to be reinstated into the Church and into the "life-germ implanted by God" which they had lost? Even from the earliest times, the Church was conscious of another power given her by

[10] Encyclical Letter of Pius XII, *Mediator Dei.* See also "Les Sacrements dans l'Economie Chrétienne," *La Maison Dieu*, No. 30, pp. 8–9; A. M. Roguet, "The Sacraments in General," in *Theological Library*, Vol. VI, *Christ in His Sacraments* (Chicago, 1957), pp. 40–44; H. De Lubac, *Catholicism* (London, 1955), p. 35.

[11] I. De la Potterie, art. cit., p. 793.

the Redeemer Himself to reconcile these fallen Christians to herself and, by her, to Christ. "By Penance and in union with the Church the sinner finds once again the peace of the Holy Spirit. In this sense, the penance of the Christian is sacramental; it is efficacious only in union with the Church and is accomplished only in an ecclesial act."[12] Christian penance is, therefore, a sacrament of *Christ in His Church.* By the visibility of the power of the keys given to the Church by Christ united with His own sorrow and avowal of sin, the Christian is certain of his forgiveness and his reincorporation into Christ and into the community of salvation which is the Church. Visible in its ministry, visible in its avowal of sin by the penitent, the sacrament of penance is the visible manifestation of Christ's saving mercy in and through the Church.

The sacrament of penance as an ecclesial act has undergone various changes in the course of the centuries. No one who has studied the penitential discipline of the third or fourth centuries can deny that certain external changes have taken place since then in the reception and the ministration of this sacrament. But neither can anyone deny that, while the external structure has changed, the essential constitution of the sacrament, the power in the Church given her by Christ to reconcile sinners, remains the same. We shall trace the notion and development of the sacrament of penance from the earliest period to the thirteenth century when it received the elaborated theological construction which has come down to us. This will be the beginning of the second section of this work. But how can the sacraments change and yet remain the same? Does not the fact that there have been certain external changes in the rite and administration of the sacrament of penance during the centuries alter the very essence of the sacrament as established by Christ? This problem will be treated in the final chapter of the second section.

But before we can really begin to understand what penance means for the Christian, we must examine the notion of sin

---

[12] Anciaux, *Le Sacrément de la Pénitence* (Louvain, 1960), p. 2.

in both the Old and New Testaments. Only a personal and loving relationship with God, tragically broken by sin, can fully explain the basic notion of penance in its total Christian context. The notions of sin and penance in Scripture are therefore essential in understanding anything of the place of penance in the economy of salvation. This will be the subject matter of the first section. It is divided into a chapter giving the basic scriptural texts which call men to do penance, two chapters on the notion of sin in Scripture, and finally a chapter on the notion of penance in Scripture both as a virtue of sinful man and as a power given to the Church. The final chapter of this section is devoted to the study of some theological reflections on sin and their relationship to the sacrament of penance.

III

We have felt for a long time that there was a great need for a small book which would combine some rudimentary scriptural, historical, and theological aspects of sin and penance. There was no such work in English and if any excuse has to be given for the present rather elementary work, let it be that someone had to begin.

PART I

Man's Infidelity: The Meaning and Reality of Sin

CHAPTER I

The Biblical Message of Sin and Penance

INTRODUCTION

The following passages are chosen from various books of the Bible. They are some of the most powerful appeals to penance and, therefore, to a conversion from sin, taken mostly from the Prophets, Christ, and the Apostles.

It was sometimes alleged, especially by liberal nineteenth-century Protestant scripture scholars, that the message of the Prophets was one of pessimism and dejection. Nothing could be farther from the truth. A simple reading of the following choice texts will clearly show that their message was one of hope and of salvation: they threatened in order to heal; entreated in order to be heard; appealed in order to be obeyed. Salvation was implicit throughout their message; it was a call to a conversion, to a *metanoia*, to a changing of direction from the path of death through sin to the way of life in God.

I. The Prophets

ISAIA

Cry out full-throated and unsparingly.
    lift up your voice like a trumpet blast;
Tell my people their wickedness
    and the house of Jacob their sins.
They seek me day after day,
    and desire to know my ways,
Like a nation that has done what is just,
    and not abandoned the law of their God;
They ask me to declare what is due them,
    pleased to gain access to God.

3

"Why do we fast, and you do not see it?
    afflict ourselves, and you take no note of it?"

Lo, on your fast day you carry out your own pursuits
    and drive all your laborers.
Yes, your fast ends in quarreling and fighting
    striking with wicked fist.
Would that today you might fast
    so as to make your voice heard on high!
Is this the manner of fasting I wish,
    of keeping a day of penance:
That a man bow his head like a reed,
    and lie in sack cloth and ashes?
Do you call this a fast,
    a day acceptable to the Lord?

This, rather, is the fasting that I wish:
    releasing those bound unjustly,
    untying the thongs of the yoke;
Setting free the oppressed,
    breaking every yoke;
Sharing your bread with the hungry,
    sheltering the oppressed and the homeless;
Clothing the naked when you see them,
    and not turning your back on your own. . . .
                                                    (Is 58:1–7)

JEREMIA

The following message came to Jeremia from the Lord: Stand at the gate of the house of the Lord, and there proclaim this message: Hear the word of the Lord, all you of Juda who enter these gates to worship the Lord! Thus says the Lord of Hosts, the God of Israel: Reform your ways and your deeds, so that I may remain with you in this place. Put not your trust in deceitful words: "This is the Temple of the Lord. The Temple of the Lord! The Temple of the Lord!" Only if you thoroughly reform your ways and your deeds; if each of you deals justly with his neighbor; if you no longer oppress the resident alien, the orphan and the widow; if you no longer shed innocent blood in this place, or follow strange gods to your own harm, will I remain with you in this place, in the land which I gave your fathers long ago and forever.

But here you are, putting your trust in deceitful words to your own loss! Are you to steal and murder, commit adultery and perjury, burn incense to Baal, go after strange gods that you know not, and yet come to stand before me in this house which bears my name, and say: "We are safe; We can commit all these abominations again"? Has this house which bears my name become in your eyes a den of thieves? I too see what is being done, says the Lord. You may go to Silo, which I made the dwelling place of my name in the beginning. See what I did to it because you have committed all these misdeeds, says the Lord, because you did not listen, though I spoke to you untiringly; because you did not answer, though I called you, I will do to this house named after me, in which you trust, and to this place which I gave to you and your fathers, just as I did to Silo. I will cast you away from me, as I cast away all your brethren, all the offspring of Ephraim.

You, now [oh Prophet], do not intercede for this people; raise not in their behalf a pleading prayer! Do not urge me, for I will not listen to you. . . .

(Jer 7:1–16)

EZECHIEL

Therefore I will judge you, house of Israel, each one according to his ways, says the Lord God. Turn and be converted from all your crimes, that they may be no cause of guilt for you. Cast away from you all the crimes you have committed, and make for yourselves a new heart and a new spirit. Why should you die, O house of Israel? For I have no pleasure in the death of anyone who dies, says the Lord God. Return and live!

(Ez 18:30 31)

As I live, says the Lord God. I swear I take no pleasure in the death of the wicked man, but rather in the wicked man's conversion, that he may live. Turn, turn, from your evil ways!

(Ez 33:11)

JOEL

Yet even now, says the Lord,
    return to me with your whole heart,
    with fasting, and weeping, and mourning;
Rend your hearts, not your garments,
    and return to the Lord, your God.
For gracious and merciful is he,
    slow to anger, rich in mercy,
    and relenting in punishment.
Perhaps he will again relent
    and leave behind him a blessing . . .

(Jl 2:12–14)

JOHN THE BAPTIST

In those days John the Baptist arrived to preach in the desert of Judea, and his theme was: "You need a change of heart; the Kingdom of Heaven is close at hand." This is the man spoken of by Isaia the prophet, who says:

> "A herald's voice rings out:
> 'Make ready the path of the Lord in the desert;
> Make straight his paths' "

. . . Soon Jerusalem and the rest of Judea, as well as the entire region on either side of the Jordan, went out to meet him. They confessed their sins and were baptized by him in the Jordan River.

On seeing many of the Pharisees and Sadducees coming to the scene of his baptism he said to them: "Brood of vipers! Who advised you to flee before the gathering storm of anger? Well, then, let your conduct show your change of heart!"

(Mt 3:1–9)

When the crowds consulted him, saying: "What, then, are we to do?" he answered them as follows: "He who has two tunics should give one to him that has none; and he who has food should do likewise."

Also tax collectors come to be baptized by him. "Rabbi," they said to him, "what are we to do?" "Exact nothing," was his answer to them, "in excess of the rate prescribed to you."

Also men of the police force consulted with him: "And for our part," they said, "what are we to do?" He replied: "Browbeat no one; blackmail no one; and be content with your pay."

(Lk 3:10–14)

II. Our Lord Jesus Christ

"Unhappy Corozain! Unhappy Bethsaida! Had the wonders done in your midst been done in Tyre and Sidon, they would long ago have repented in sack cloth and ashes. At all events, it will go less hard on Judgment Day with Tyre and Sidon then with you."

(Mt 11:21–22)

". . . those eighteen persons whom the Tower at the Pool of Siloam crushed to death by its fall — do you suppose they were worse offenders than the rest of the inhabitants of Jerusalem? No indeed, I assure you; in fact, if you do not mend your evil ways, you will, everyone of you, likewise perish."

(Lk 13:4–5)

"I tell you, there is joy in heaven over one repentant sinner
— more, in fact, than over ninety-nine saints that have no need
of repentance."

(Lk 15:7)

"If they do not listen to Moses and the Prophets, neither will
they be convinced if a dead man rises."

(Lk 16:31)

"This," he said to them, "is the sense of the Scriptures: The
Messias must suffer and on the third day rise from the dead.
Furthermore: in his name repentance and forgiveness of sins must
be preached to all the nations. . . ."

(Lk 24:46–47)

III. The Apostles

PETER

"Repent, therefore, and be converted, that your sins may be
blotted out. . . ."

(Acts 3:19)

PAUL

"I take it for granted that you have hearkened to him [Christ]
and have been taught in him, since truth is in Jesus. You are
to put off your old self, with its former habits, which is on the
road to ruin as its deceptive lusts deserve. Renew yourselves constantly by spiritual considerations, and put on the new self,
created after the image of God in the justice and holiness that
come from truth."

(Eph 4:20–24)

JOHN

"If we should say that we are not guilty of sin, we deceive
ourselves, and the light of truth is not within us. If we openly
confess our sins, God, true to his promises and just, forgives
us our sins and cleanses us from every stain of iniquity. If we
should say that we have never been guilty of sin, we make him
a liar, and his message does not dwell within us. My little children, I write this letter to you to keep you from sin. Yet if anyone
should commit a sin, we have an advocate with the Father,
Jesus Christ, the holy One. He himself is the propitiation for
our sins; indeed, not only for ours, but for those of the whole
world."

(1 Jn 1:8–10; 2:1)

CHAPTER II

Sin in the Old Testament

INTRODUCTION

The theme of sin is one of the central and most encompassing of all the Old Testament revelations.[1] Throughout the course of the sacred history of the Jews sin runs as a main thread to reveal the central preoccupation of the sacred authors: God wills to save man from sin. The various notions of sin in the Old Testament, its universality, its origin, its relationship between God and His people,[2] are topics constantly recurring. Indeed, it is this personal relationship which explains the deep tragedy of sin in Israel, for sin is the very element which destroys this relationship. Nothing could be further from the Old Testament notion of sin than the impersonal notion of sin among the Greeks.[3] Strictly speaking, the Greeks did not know sin because they knew of no personal relationship with God. The prime mover of Aristotle's metaphysics did not care in the least about humanity, self-satisfied as he was with his own contemplation and happiness. The perspective for the Greeks was intellectual more than existential sin, for the goodness or badness of human action was measured by its alignment or nonalignment with intelligence.[4] The Old Testament, on the contrary, conceived of human action as a personal relationship with a God who was

---

[1] J. Guillet, *Themes of the Bible* (Notre Dame, 1960), p. 103. See also A. Gelin, *Key Concepts of the Old Testament* (New York, 1957), p. 66; S. Lyonnet, *De Peccato et Redemptione*, I (Romae, 1957), pp. 27–51.

[2] J. Guillet, *op. cit.*, p. 100.

[3] H. Rondet, *The Theology of Sin* (Notre Dame, 1960), p. 6; A. Jagu, "Les Philosophes Grecs," in *Théologie du Péché* (Tournai, 1960), p. 238. See illuminating study of sin in the Old Testament from a historical approach in L. Ligier, *Péché d'Adam et Péché du Monde* (Paris, 1960), 2 vols.

[4] A. Jagu, *art. cit.*, *Théologie* . . . , p. 213.

intensely interested in the people He dealt with. An action was good or bad, and therefore virtuous or sinful, because God said so and for no other reason. Sin, in this context, was refusal to respond to God's initiative and love. For the Greeks, sin never reached beyond an error, an ignorance, or a madness that led to man's self-destruction. This notion of the intensely personal relationship between God and man must be kept firmly in mind if we wish to form a correct notion of sin in the Old Testament.

As a matter of fact, it is absolutely impossible to understand the whole mystery of salvation as found in the Judeo-Christian revelation without this basic notion. In a sense, then, the Greek notion of sin went as far as it could in understanding what it was for man; but for them it was absurd to think that the gods could have an intense interest and personal relationship with man.[5] In this sense, then, the notion of sin as we know it today, or as the Jews of old knew it, could only be a consequence and product of God's revelation of Himself to men.[6]

Vocabulary of Sin.[7] The word most commonly used in the Old Testament to express the notion of sin is *HT'* which the Greek Bible translates as *hamartia.* Literally, it means to miss the mark or to fall away from a known path or way. Applied morally, it means to be deceived or led astray. The general idea it conveys is a lack of some element in attaining a desired end. Thus we read in Isaia 65:20:

> He dies a mere youth who reaches but a hundred years,
> and he who fails of a hundred shall be thought accursed.

When applied to the notion of sin in the Bible, it takes on the meaning of a failing toward someone, a violation of a bond which unites persons to each other and thus injures the person

---

[5] C. H. Dodd, *The Greeks and the Bible* (London, 1954), pp. 64–78.

[6] E. Jacob, *Theology of the Old Testament* (London, 1958), p. 284; W. Eichrodt, *Theology of the Old Testament,* I (Philadelphia, 1960), pp. 472–501.

[7] P. Van Imschoot, *Théologie de l'Ancien Testament,* II (Tournai, 1957), pp. 278–282; J. J. Von Allmen, ed., *Vocabulary of the Bible* (London, 1961), pp. 405–407.

against whom the bond was broken.[8] This takes on all the
aspects of an intimate personal relationship between two people,
one of whom has injured the other by breaking a personal tie
which united the two. When Jephte sent messengers to the
King of the Ammonites, he protested, saying, "I have not sinned
against you, but you wrong me by warring against me" (Jgs
11:27. See also Gn 20:9 and 1 Sm 26:21). But *hamartia* takes
on a truly poignant meaning when it expresses a personal failing
toward God. David, of course, is a great example of this when
and after he is accused of adultery by the prophet Nathan (2
Sm 12:13). David realizes that he has broken the intimate relationship between himself and God. Thus in Psalm 51, which is
attributed to David himself, the poignant phrase appears:

> Against You only have I sinned.

The rest of the Psalm is a description of the Psalmist's sorrow
but the essential factor remains unchanged: he has offended
Yahweh personally.[9]

Finally this same root *HT'* is used to express the notion of
man's failure to live up to the will of God. Man, by his sin,
misses the destiny which God has established for him. In a very
true sense, sin is not only a failing in a personal relationship
with God, it is, as a consequence, a failing of our destined end
which can only lead to death and self-destruction:

> For he who finds me finds life
>   and wins favor from the Lord.
> But he who misses me harms himself;
>   all who hate me love death (Prv 8:35).

The second word used almost as frequently as *HT'* is the
Hebrew *'awon*, which describes the interior state of the guilty
man. It denotes the disorder and the interior deviation which
sin causes in the life of man. It is, perhaps, what we would call
remorse of conscience, a remorse which tortures the man who
has offended God. It is a great weight which bears down con-

---

[8] J. Guillet, *op. cit.*, p. 102.
[9] H. Rondet, *op. cit.*, p. 14.

tinuously on the sinner. The Jews of old, therefore, attempted to transfer this burden of guilt from themselves to the scapegoat (Lv 26:22).[10] Even more striking is this substitution of sin (which was not considered to be fictitious) from the people to the Levitical priesthood, officially charged as it was to make offering and satisfaction for the sins of the people: ". . . Aaron bears whatever guilt the Israelites may incur in consecrating any of their sacred gifts . . ." (Ex 28:38). As a consequence of this burden and consciousness of guilt and sin, man must die. Death is the consequence of sin (Gn 15:17; Sir 35:23; and Wis 2:24).

Origin of Sin. As revealed to us throughout the pages of the Old Testament man is the origin of sin. In tone and construction, the sacred author of Genesis gives us a popular account of the creation of the universe and of man. God created man to be happy if he would obey; but man chose to follow his own self-will, and this resulted in death for himself and his posterity and the loss of the intimacy he enjoyed with God. It is interesting to note the difference between the biblical account of man's creation and fall with that of the diverse fables of the Babylonians. In the Bible, man is created free, and he is created by God to enjoy the goods God has given him. In Babylonian literature, the freedom of man, as well as his happiness, is the envy of the gods who manage to steal it from him.[11] Man's death and unhappiness are thus explained, in this context, as the result of involuntary and hostile forces. How more beautiful and real is the biblical narration! Man is created in God's image:

> God created man in his image.
> In the image of God he created him (Gn 1:27).

Adam is a prototype of all humanity. This was seen clearly by

---

[10] Even more striking is the only *personal* element of vicarious suffering in the Old Testament: the suffering servant in Isaia 40:1–9; 49:1–9ª; 50:49; 52:13–53:12 where the literary unit is one. This is probably the only case in the Old Testament where we find a man suffering for the people. See V. de Leeuw, "Le Serviteur de Jahvé," in *L'Attente du Messie* (Tournai, 1954), pp. 51–56; W. Zimmerli, *The Servant of God* (Naperville, Ill., 1957), pp. 9–34.

[11] P. Pritchard, *Ancient Near East Texts* (Princeton, N. J., 1954), p. 123.

the *Apocalypse of Baruch:* "Each of us is Adam for himself"
(54:19). Thus under the type of Adam and Eve, which, of
course, does not exclude their historical reality, the origin of
sin by disobedience to God's commandment is portrayed; and
because Adam and Eve are the prototypes of humanity, the
author represents all men in sin through their sin. This parallel
is brilliantly set out for us by St. Paul, who shows that just as
all men were engulfed in sin by Adam's sin (Paul calls Adam
a "type"), so Christ, by His obedience, establishes the kingdom of
universal salvation:

> Therefore, as through one man sin entered into the world and
> through sin death, and thus death has spread to all men in whom
> all have sinned. . . . For if by reason of the one man's offense
> death reigned through the one man, much more will they who
> receive the abundance of the grace and of the gift of holiness
> reign in life through the one Jesus Christ (Rom 5:12, 17).[12]

Man has not only constituted himself a sinner by his own
transgression, but all men are in some way mysteriously involved
in sin, which has some connection with the sin of Adam. We
do not find the idea of original sin in the Old Testament as
such (this will be brought out more fully by St. Paul), but what
we do find is that the sacred author teaches that all men are
involved in sin through Adam's fall.[13] "The inclination of man's
heart is evil from his youth" (Gn 8:21), but only Sir 21 explicitly establishes a relationship between the sins of all men and
that of Adam. In the Old Testament there is a mysterious
solidarity among men in sin (see Ez 36:20; Ps 50:7; Jb 14:1–6).
As the Psalmist says,

> Indeed, in guilt was I born,
>   and in sin my mother conceived me (Ps 50:7).

The teaching is certainly not that of original sin but rather a
practical observation by the Psalmist that man sins even from

---

[12] See for this relationship: L. Cerfaux, *Christ in the Theology of Saint Paul* (New York, 1959), pp. 85–86.

[13] Ch. Boyer, "Péché Originel," in *Théologie du Péché,* p. 42; C. Spicq, "Men's sin," in *The God of Israel, the God of Christians* (New York, 1961), pp. 149–163.

his earliest days. It is a sort of cosmic apprehension of man's evil and sin, and his personal involvement in it from the first days of his youth.[14]

The origins of sin, therefore, are to be found in man himself, in his personal revolt against a God who is personally involved with him. The two elements of the mysterious origins of man's sin evolve throughout the Old Testament: Adam's sin and the rest of mankind's mysterious connection with it. And as a result of this man finds himself in some sort of evil state from his earliest days. The concepts are admittedly obscure as are many other religious concepts of the Old Testament, for the full malice of sin as well as the origins of original sin in and through Adam were reserved for full revelation in the New Testament. St. Paul would explain the latter, and only the crucifixion and resurrection of the Word Incarnate would give man the full and final answer to sin in its personal relationship of love to God.[15]

Universality of Sin. This notion follows from the fact that all men are mysteriously involved with the type-sinner who was Adam. This notion is expanded in the whole progress of salvation contained in the sacred books of the Bible. After Adam's sin, individual sins multiply at an ever increasing rate. Man's brutality and callousness is heard in the voice of Lamech:

> I kill a man for wounding me,
>   a youth for bruising me;
> If Cain shall be avenged sevenfold,
>   Lamech, seventy times sevenfold (Gn 4:23–24).

Thus the popular narrative of Genesis brings us to a sort of universal contamination: ". . . The Lord saw that the wickedness of man on the earth was great, and that man's every thought and all the inclination of his heart were only evil . . ." (Gn 6:5). God destroys man whom He created except for Noe who found favor with Him (Gn 6:9–8:22). But the sinfulness of

---

[14] E. Jacob, *op. cit.*, p. 287.

[15] A. Gelin, "Le Péché dans l'Ancien Testament," in *Théologie du Péché*, p. 42.

man did not stop, and the pride of the men who built the Tower of Babel is once again punished by God (Gn 11:1–9). It is to be noted, however, that for each such manifestation of evil, God's mercy responds with an act of forgiveness and a promise of salvation (Gn 3:15; 8:20, etc.). It was the same with the Patriarchs. To the blessing of Abraham (Gn 12:2) corresponds the universal curse of Adam, and by and through Abraham, we have the beginnings of God's promise of universal salvation.[16] God chooses a people to whom He reveals Himself as protector and guide; He promises them benediction if they will follow His commandments (Ex 34:10–13). But the entire history of the Chosen People is one of sin and infidelity to the God "Who had called them from the land of slavery, Egypt," and a return to the slavery of sin from which God had called them. This becomes a constant theme with the prophets, who see in Israel's sins a return to Egypt, i.e., to a spiritual state of slavery (Ez 16:26; 20:8; 21:29).

> They shall not dwell in the Lord's land;
> Ephraim shall return to Egypt,
> and in Assyria they shall eat unclean food (Os 9:3).

But God continues to save a chosen few who become His protected ones, known as the Poor of Yahweh or "the rest" in the terms of Isaia.[17] These are faithful to God through the purification of the desert and the Babylonian Exile, and from them stem the future Christians who do not come "from the Israel of the flesh but of God" (Gal 6:16). This is St. Paul's argument in the famous passage in the Epistle to the Romans (9:1–11:35) where he shows that the privileges of Israel as the Chosen People were but temporary dispositions and that the more profound intention of God was the "Israel of God" who would believe in Christ, the object of all the promises made by God to "Abraham and his seed forever."[18]

The prophets continue this line of thought by showing that

---

[16] Van Imschoot, *op. cit.*, pp. 296–297.

[17] A. Gelin, *Les Pauvres de Yahvé* (Paris, 1953), pp. 16–23.

[18] L. Cerfaux, *The Church in the Theology of Saint Paul*, pp. 59–66.

the Israelites were no better than the Gentiles because they were unfaithful to God's commandments. The theme of the "uncircumcised heart" is revealing in this regard. True circumcision is of the heart; that is, it is a quality of the heart and mind which obeys the commandments of God (Jer 4:4; 9:25; Dt 10:26; 30:5). This same theme is resumed in the famous dossier of St. Paul where he proves that all men are sinners, whether they be Jews or Gentiles:

> What then? Are we better off than the Gentiles? Not entirely. For we have just charged that Jews and Greeks are all under the domination of sin, as it is written,
> "There is not one just man;
> There is none who understands" (Rom 3:9-10).

It is interesting to note that St. Paul's passage assembles most of the interesting and revealing texts of the Old Testament with regard to the universal condition of sinful man (Ps 14:1-2; 52:2-4; Sir 7:20; Is 59:7; Lv 1:79; Gn 2:16; 3:22; 6:12; Prv 1:16). Thus from the very beginning, the Old Testament continuously displayed the universal sinful state of man, be he Jew or Gentile.

Sin and the Alliance. Sin, say the prophets, is an attempt on the heart of God. This intensely personal and living experience between Yahweh and the people came from the fact that God voluntarily chose Israel as His own to the exclusion of all others.

"Thus says the Lord, 'Israel is my son, my first born'" (Ex 4:22). The use of the words "Son," "kingdom of Priests," "Chosen People," "Father" are not fictitious, but actually imply a bond of voluntarily established, reciprocal, and loving obligations:

> You shall be my special possession, dearer to me than all other people, though all the earth is mine. You shall be to me a kingdom of priests, a holy nation (Ex 19:5-6).

Because of this, God was deeply wounded whenever Israel abandoned Him for other gods. In contrast, the prophet Osee uses the loving image of the wife-husband for the relationship between God and Israel:

I will espouse you to me forever:
I will espouse you in right and in justice,
   in love and in mercy (Os 2:21).

The dialogue of this same love (the Covenant), which has been
shamefully disregarded by Israel, is continued:

Protest against your mother, protest!
   for she is not my wife,
   and I am not her husband.
Let her remove her harlotry from before her,
   her adultery from between her breasts;
Or I will strip her naked,
   leaving her as on the day of her birth;
. . . I will have no pity on her children (Os 2:4–6).

The conjugal relationship between Yahweh and Israel has been
broken. In this sense, Israel "knows" Yahweh, that is, has an
intimate and living knowledge of Him in the Covenant which
Israel disregards to her own destruction (Os 13:14; 2:21). All
this stems from the living — one would say today, existential —
experience that the prophets had of God. Their experience was
that Israel and the alliance are seen as a marriage and sin as the
adultery of the Chosen People[19] (Ex 34:6). The testimony of
the prophet Osee is especially striking. Osee sees the whole relationship between God and Israel based on an allegory of his
own marriage. His wife left him to mix with others. In a similar
vein, the whole of the relationship between Israel and God is
seen in the light of this bad marriage and unfaithful wife.

What is also important in the personal notion of the sin
covenant is the obligation to love one's neighbor. Now it is
obvious that the term "neighbor" meant one's own kin or another
member of the Chosen People.[20] It did not as yet have that
expansive and universal meaning it was to receive only with
the coming of Christ. But the alliance did suppose obligations at
least toward the fellow members of the Chosen People. In minia-
ture form, this relationship is similar to the more perfect union

---

[19] A. Gelin, art. cit., *Théologie* . . . , pp. 33–34.
[20] A. Grail, "Love of my Neighbor: An Essay in Biblical Theology," in
Love of Our Neighbor (Springfield, Ill., 1955), pp. 6–9.

of Christians with each other in Christ. The reasoning in the
Old Testament was that since they were all the beloved of
God as a nation, to love God was also to love one's neighbor.
Speaking of the man who treated his neighbor well, Jeremia says:

> Because he dispensed justice to the weak and the poor,
>   it went well with him.
> Is this not true knowledge of me?
>   says the Lord (Jer 22:16).

Leviticus is even more forceful. After explaining the diverse
obligations of the Covenant and its laws, God commands the
Chosen People (as a consequence of this very Covenant):

> Take no revenge and cherish no grudge against your fellow coun-
> trymen. You shall love your neighbor as yourself. I am the Lord
> (Lv 19:18).

All this, it is evident, is greatly expanded by the revelation of
Christ, but the personalistic relationship of love between God
and His People and between the People themselves is already
present in the Old Testament.[21] The social aspects of sin that
are so important for a correct notion of sin in the New Testament are already present in the Old.

Conversion, Expiation, and Pardon of Sin. The call to conversion is a constant theme in all of the prophets. As a matter
of fact, this was one of their main objectives for being sent by
God: to warn the Jewish people to come back (to be converted)
before it is too late:

> And, now, tell this to the men of Juda and the citizens of
> Jerusalem: Thus says the Lord: Take care. I am fashioning evil
> against you and making a plan. Return, each of you, from his
> evil way; reform your ways and your deeds (Jer 18:11; see also
> 25:5).

The word "conversion" as a noun is found nowhere in the
Old Testament, for in the light of the Old Testament revelation
there is no such thing as a "converted" man. There is only the
notion of a man who is continuously converting his ways in

---

[21] *The Book of Jeremia*, Part I with a commentary by N. M. Flanagan
(Pamphlet Bible Series), p. 16.

God's love and in His commandments.[22] Such things as disappointments and sorrow, even tragedy, can be the occasion whereby a person begins to "rethink his ways" and to begin this conversion to God from his evil ways. It was in this connection that Ezechiel was to see good come from the terrible Babylonian Captivity of 586 B.C.

> I will make you plunder for the nations. I will cut you off from the peoples, and remove you from the lands. I will destroy you, and thus you shall know that I am the Lord (Ez 25:7).

Expiation and pardon of sin are implied in the appeal for conversion and repentance.[23] When man recognizes his fault for what it is, a personal affront to God, then God is full of "mercy for those who seek him." The Psalmist addresses himself to God's mercy when he says:

> Have mercy on me, O God, in your goodness;
>   in the greatness of your compassion wipe out my offense
>   (Ps 50:1).

But expiation must be the product of man's free will, not an exterior rite with no effect on the interior man.[24] True repentance and expiation must proceed from the heart of man; above all, it must be interior. As the Psalmist expresses it,

> My sacrifice, O God, is a contrite spirit;
>   a heart contrite and humbled, O God, you will not spurn
>   (Ps 50:19).

This exteriorization of the cult was the constant fault of the Jews of the Old Testament.[25] The prophets bear abundant testimony on this point:

> What care I for the number of your sacrifices?
>   says the Lord.

---

[22] A. Glein, *art. cit., Théologie* . . . , p. 42; J. Pierron, "Conversion: the Return to God," in *The God of Israel, the God of Christians* (New York, 1961), pp. 164–173.

[23] P. Anciaux, *Le Sacrément de la Pénitence* (Louvain, 1960), p. 12.

[24] Th. C. Vriezen, *An Outline of Old Testament Theology* (Oxford, 1960), p. 210.

[25] H. W. Robinson, *The Cross in the Old Testament* (London, 1960), p. 111.

> I have had enough of whole-burnt rams
>   and fat of fatlings;
> In the blood of calves, lambs and goats
>   I find no pleasure (Is 1:11; see also Jer 11:15; Lam 5:6; Is 63:7;
>   Dn 9:8).

What then was the usefulness of the sacrifices which are reported on practically every page of the Old Testament? Sacrifice
is a means by which man expresses (by a substitute) his total
submission to God and to which God responds by a communication of His life. It was because sacrifices were not offered in this
spirit that God so often rejected them.

The ultimate tragedy of Israel is told in the prophet Jeremia.
God's mercy has been rejected so often that only the complete
destruction of Israel as a race will suffice to expiate its sin. But
even here, God's mercy and pardon of sin are not lost. God can
give back life to dead bodies just as He can give back life to
Israel which was dead in its exile. This is the meaning of the
great vision of the dry bones in the prophecy of Ezechiel:

> Dry bones, hear the word of the Lord! Thus says the Lord
> God to these bones: See, I will bring spirit into you, that you
> may come to life. I will put sinews upon you, make flesh grow
> over you, cover you with skin, and put spirit into you so that you
> may come to life and know that I am the Lord (37.5-7).

This analogy of death-life by God's word is a constant theme
in the Old and New Testaments. Sin produces only the kingdom
of death, of misery, and of destruction. By heeding God's word
(His commandments) a man is brought from this spiritual death
to God's life and light. Obviously, the reception of God's word
as a destruction of death in man is only an imperfect revelation
of the reception by men of God's substantial Word which in
the New Testament becomes the Word Incarnate.[26]

Conclusion

The Old Testament is a massive denunciation of sin as an
offense to God. The doctrine is rather imperfect and awaits its

---

[26] E. Jacob, *op. cit.*, pp. 132–133; J. Szeruda, *Das Wort Jahwes*, p. 126.

perfect completion in the New Testament with the coming of Christ. Here, and only here, can the complete understanding of the offense which sin really is to a loving and merciful God be gained. Only here can the logic of sin as revealed in the Old Testament be fully understood. Yet the Old Testament demonstrates the essence of sin: on the supernatural plane, sin is a refusal of God; on the human plane, it is a perversion of man himself. By refusing God, man also refuses himself. It is for this reason that the notion of conversion holds such a prominent place in the Old Testament. By conversion and by conversion alone does a man realize the exact dimension of sin, its religious dimension, because conversion places man directly before God.[27]

[27] A. Gelin, art. cit., *Théologie* . . . , p. 42.

CHAPTER III

Sin in the New Testament

INTRODUCTION

"The work of the theologian, as that of the exegete, will always be to state as objectively as possible — without ever forcing the texts out of a polemic concern — the progressive action, humanly pedagogical, of God in communicating the great truths of His revelations to the thoughts of men both as individuals and as groups."[1] This principle of modern scriptural study will come as a shock only to those who have not followed the great lines of scriptural development over the past 50 years. This development cannot be neglected in this present study of the notion of sin in the New Testament. The thought of Christ, that of the primitive Christian community, and the developed theology of St. John and St. Paul will each have its manner of approaching the tremendous reality of sin in Christian life. Yet one thing remains fundamental throughout all the writings of the New Testament: sin is a drama between two persons, a personal and intimate relationship. Modern atheism is a thing unknown to the *homo biblicus*; he was very conscious of this personal relationship between himself and God. This relationship has been broken by sin.[2] "Man was, for the writers of the New Testament, created for fellowship with God; man has broken this fellowship. This is his sin. In Christ we have God's forgiveness made incarnate for men, which men must choose or reject."[3] The early Greeks never

---

[1] J. Levie, "Interprétation Scripturaire," in *Sacra Pagina,* I (Louvain, 1960), p. 118.

[2] See *supra,* p. 15.

[3] W. Grundmann, "Sin in the New Testament," in *Key Bible Words,* ed. J. R. Coates (taken from *Wörterbuch Zum Neuen Testament,* G. Kittel), p. 67.

came to such a personal and intimate relationship with God. Christianity is the sinner's religion. The sinner stands before God.[4] And above all, the writers of the New Testament present the fact that in Christ the holiness of God is the judging of sin, and in Christ the love of God is the saving of the sinner. The Greeks or the heathen world could not even conceive of this ideal. As a matter of fact, "a mystery which offered the remission of sins would have been a monstrosity to the Greeks."[5] This was the great innovation of the Christian message, and in the words of St. Peter, "Jesus charged us to preach to the people and to bear witness that it is he who has been appointed by God to be judge of the living and the dead. To him all the prophets bear witness that through his name all who believe in him may receive forgiveness of sins" (Acts 10:42–43).

In the following pages the essential message of God's revelation addressed to men for the forgiveness of sin is developed in two major phases. The first phase is the message given by Christ Himself, which is not as fully developed a theology as that of the Apostles John and Paul. This development is not to be wondered at, for God, even in the Scriptures, accommodates Himself to the minds of His people. The fundamental notion of sin and conversion is consistent throughout the New Testament, even if more theologically developed in St. John and St. Paul.[6] This will be the second phase of our investigation. Only by examining the total context of the New Testament can the riches of the notion of sin and its necessary counterpart, salvation and justice, be seen. In this context alone will we be able to see "the true measure of Jesus' conception of sin."[7]

---

[4] G. Kittel, *Die Lebenskrafte der Ersten Christlichen Gemeinden*, pp. 19–22.

[5] K. Holl, "Urchristentum und Religionsgeschichte," in *Zeitschr. für Theol. Syst.*, 32 (1924), 339–342.

[6] See A. Descamps, "La Methode en Théologie Biblique," in *Sacra Pagina*, Vol. I, pp. 138–143.

[7] A. Descamps, "Le Péché dans le Nouveau Testament," in *Théologie du Péché* (Tournai, 1960), p. 52.

I. Preliminary Remarks

1. In the Old Testament, sin was not only the destruction of the personal relationship between man and God, but also by that very fact a destruction of the relationship of man with his fellow man. Sin was the divisive factor which separated man both from God and from the rest of nature (Gn 3:17–18).[8] In other words, sin was social in nature as well as individual in origin (in a negative vein) (Jer 8:20; 27:18). This element of solidarity was especially evident in the sins of the leaders of Israel: kings, priests, and prophets. The New Testament strongly emphasized this social element of sin. In the words of St. Paul, the Christian people form one body, and when one member suffers (by sin) then all the members suffer and are to come to his aid. The element of mutual charity and, therefore, of mutual involvement in the damage and pain caused by another Christian's sin is so strong that it may well be the very definition of the Christian while he awaits the second coming of Christ.[9] In this regard, fraternal correction is a form of Christian charity and a concern over the final welfare of the sinner in question.

New Testament terminology is striking in its connection between sin and charity. A sin or fault now incurs a debt as well as an injury toward the neighbor. In Mk 6:12, this is evident in the use of the Greek *opheiletes*, a term stressing a debt we owe our neighbor which we have incurred by our sin. This

---

[8] See the commentary on this passage by A. Clamer, *La Sainte Bible de Pirot: La Génèse*, Vol. I (Paris, 1953), pp. 149–154.

[9] *Theologisches Wörterbuch Zum Neuen Testament*, Band I, pp. 310–311. "Charity is the achievement of the celestial realities, for God is Charity, present and realizing His presence. It is in this sense that the charity of God is made perfect in him who keeps the word of Christ (1 Jn 2:5) when we love one another (1 Jn 4:12)." L. Cerfaux, "La Charité Fraternelle et le Rétour du Christ," in *Recueil Lucien Cerfaux* Vol. II, p. 37. For forgiveness of neighbor in New Testament see A. Descamps, *Les Justes et la Justice dans les Evangiles*, pp. 137–138; R. E. Brown, "The Pater Noster as an Eschatological Prayer," in *Theological Studies*, 22 (June, 1961), pp. 199–203.

phrase is found in the finest Christian prayer, the "Our Father."[10]
As a matter of fact, there is a specific relationship set up between
the forgiveness of our sins by God and the forgiveness by one
Christian of the sins of another. In the measure that we forgive
each other, to that degree God forgives us. In still other passages,
this particular aspect of mutual love in forgiveness is also brought
out in relationship to the divinity itself (Mt 18:15; Lk 17:3-4;
Gal 6:1). This is certainly the great lesson of the parable of the
wicked servant who refused to forgive his fellow servant in spite
of the fact that the master had already forgiven him so much
more (Mt 18:23-35). Our forgiveness is measured in direct
proportion to our forgiveness for one another.[11]

2. As in the Old Testament, but to a much greater degree, sin
in the New Testament becomes a drama enacted between two
persons who are engaged in the closest bonds of union. "God is,
in the Bible and particularly in the New Testament, a living and
personal being who without ceasing takes the initiative to meet
His people, to offer them His benefits and to ask their fidelity in
return. Two ways are open to the people: if they choose attachment to God, they will share in divine goods; but if they choose
revolt and sin — for man can always turn against God — they
hold in check the salvific design of God."[12] This personal God
has thus gone as far as He could possibly go to reconcile man
to Himself by sending His only-begotten Son who is the Love
of God incarnate for men (Jn 1:14). With Him, the Kingdom
of God has made its entrance in time on earth. God has personally and definitively intervened through His own begotten
Son (Heb 1:2). Sin is an injustice which troubles the peace of
the Kingdom and provokes the wrath of God. This theme domi-
nates the whole of the New Testament.[13] The personal element

---

[10] A. Lefevre, "Péché et Pénitence dans la Bible," in La Maison Dieu,
1958, no. 55, p. 17.

[11] Wörterbuch Zum Neuen Testament, loc. cit., p. 306. This is also the
tradition of the Fathers of the Church, cf. St. Cyprian, De Oratione Do-
minica (CSEL, 3, 1), 265-294.

[12] A. Descamps, art. cit., Théologie . . . , p. 55.

[13] A. Lefevre, art. cit., La Maison Dieu . . . , p. 7.

in sin as a disturbance of the Kingdom is brought out by the description of sin as an infidelity which wounds the love of God as would the infidelity of a beloved spouse.[14] Even more expressive in this personal relationship between man and God are the parables of the lost sheep and the prodigal son. All these metaphors and anthropomorphisms must be understood in their context; while it is true that God can never really be touched by sin, they do serve to illustrate the refusal, which is sin, toward a personal God who loves the sinner and continuously seeks him out to bring him back to the fold and to "the Father's House."

3. "Without faith in God, the all powerful Father and creator, without faith in His redemptive love, it is impossible to have any sense of sin. The consciousness of sin supposes faith in the personal relations between God, whose transcendent holiness goes together with His infinite love; and men who are invited by Him to participate in His Community of life and love which is the Holy Trinity."[15] Modern man's preoccupation with reducing sin to a result of malfunction of public order, psychological deviations, etc., is the negation of liberty and human responsibility and therefore of the very notion of sin itself. Nothing could be further from the conception of personal guilt and responsibility in the *homo biblicus*. In the Bible, man is free and responsible for his actions before God Himself. This concept is taken for granted in practically all the books of the Bible. The universal call of repentance by the prophets, Christ, and the Apostles is implicitly based on this responsibility.[16] The sinner must return to God or be punished. One of the few, even though one of the most striking analyses of the interior state of the sinner, is given by St. Paul in Rom 7:14, where he speaks of the struggle between what is right (God's law) and what Paul does (sin).

This free act, when it repeats itself often enough, goes from an individual transgression, which is serious enough, into something more dreadful: a state of sin. This sinful condition of all humanity

---

[14] *Ibid.*, p. 9.
[15] P. Anciaux, *Le Sacrément de la Pénitence* (Louvain, 1960), p. 6.
[16] See appropriate texts cited above, pp. 3–7.

under whose curse man has lain prostrate since the time of Adam's first transgression has grown by the subsequent personal sins of men (Rom 5:17–19).[17] Our modern vocabulary has kept some of these biblical notions when it speaks of someone "being in the state of sin" or "leading a life of sin." And so man's state of sin overflows into his very social structures wherein the sinner is enveloped on every side, and which, in its turn, leads to further sin and blindness. It is this terrible state of man that St. Paul so poignantly describes.[18] The biblical doctrine of sin is not mythological but historical. Sin, for the man of the Bible, is a fact of experience which he cannot deny and which develops out of his own liberty.

This notion of sin, however, should not lead us into pessimism. Although sin brings its own punishment in a sentiment of culpability (Gn 3:14–15) and although by sinning man breaks away from God (Jn 9:31), the God of mercies is still rich to those who recognize what they have done and return. This is clearly seen in the suffering servant who "takes away" sin in God's name. The motive here, however, is different from that of the Old Testament; the return to God in the New Testament is out of love in the Father-Son relationship established in and through Christ.[19]

II. Sin in the Message of Jesus

1. The notion of the Kingdom's presence in the person of Christ is fundamental to any comprehension of the Synoptic Gospels. "The forgiveness proclaimed and practiced by Jesus is something new and extraordinary. It is the defeat of sin, the breaking in of the Kingdom of God, an eschatological event."[20]

---

[17] L. Cerfaux, *Une Lecture de l'Epître aux Romains* (Tournai, 1947), pp. 58–61.

[18] A. Kirchagassner, *Erlösung und Sünde im Neuen Testament*, pp. 253–262.

[19] J. Guillet, *Themes of the Bible* (Notre Dame, 1960), p. 100; S. Lyonnet, *De Peccato et de Redemptione*, I, pp. 39–40.

[20] Walter Grundmann, "Sin in the New Testament," in *Key Bible Words*, pp. 66–67; S. Lyonnet, *De Peccato et Redemptione*, II (Romae, 1960), 97–117.

This new epoch is evident in the opening chapter of St. Matthew's Gospel on the beginning of the public ministry of Christ. "Repent, for the Kingdom of heaven is at hand." The terms "Kingdom of heaven," "brood of vipers," "the wrath to come," "thrown into the fire," "winnowing fork," and "unquenchable fire" are all biblical terms referring to man's last end. They are eschatological. In the minds of the evangelists, there is no doubt that the coming of Christ was the beginning of the establishment of the Kingdom, the beginning of the last times of judgment and salvation.[21] It will culminate and end with the second coming of Christ or the Parousia. Meanwhile, life is a time of tension, of trial, of repentance. God in His mercy gives the present time between the Incarnation and the Parousia as a period of repentance for sinners: "Do penance, for the kingdom of heaven is close at hand" (Mt 4:17; see also Mk 1:15). Referring to the first three petitions of the Synoptic Gospels in the *Our Father*, a famous author says: "What animates these petitions? It is the Parousia. The second is central and the first and third bring more light upon it. The kingdom is already present but it is also to come. It is a grace because it comes from God but it is also a demand on our part because we have been transformed for life in the Kingdom and we must live accordingly. It obliges us to a new service — to sanctify. . . . The celestial aspect is already present in us but in an imperfect way."[22] Hence the need for a continuous conversion and repentance to make ourselves more worthy both of our present status as sons in this Kingdom, which has started on earth with Christ and His Church, and of the complete revelation of this kingdom at the Parousia.

In this regard, note the flight of the demons who expect the judgment which will render them powerless. They are tortured by the presence of Christ in whom they already recognize the

---

[21] L. Cerfaux, *The Four Gospels* (Westminster, Md., 1960), pp. 37–38.
[22] J. Jacquenier, "Le Notre Père," in *Eph. Théo. Lov.*, 34 (July–August, 1949), pp. 74–79.

presence of the Kingdom and therefore of the judgment.[23] "Have you come here to torment us before the appointed time?" (Mt 8:29; Mk 5:7; Lk 8:28.)[24]

In Christ we have the divine pity which forces back the realm of evil and sin. We witness this whole tendency in the many exorcisms that Christ performs as well as in the miracles. Let us examine the miracle of the curing of the paralytic (Mt 9:1–8). For the Jews of old, sickness of body was always the consequence of sin, so when a man was healed, he had first to be cleansed spiritually, and then as a consequence of this, his physical cure followed. Christ corrected this view for it was not entirely correct (Jn 9:2–3). But at the same time, Christ, in a general way, accommodates Himself to His listeners and to a certain extent to this Jewish thought.[25] This is true in the cure of the paralytic. Christ forgives the man's sins and then and only then — so that the Jews would be fully convinced of the efficacy of Christ's power to forgive sin — He cures his body. In this way, the physical cure becomes the proof of Christ's power over sin.[26] The Kingdom of God has thus descended upon earth in the form of Christ, who, in reference to Dn 7:8, speaks of Himself as the famous "Son of Man" who establishes God's Kingdom on earth.[27] The definitive form of the Kingdom is for the future just as the definitive destruction of sin is for the future; but the radical possibility for man to overcome sin and the demonic powers in whose power he is held captive is given to us by the presence of Christ who is the appearance among men of heavenly gifts. Sin in its definitive form attacks Jesus and the Kingdom. The sinner refuses God's love as it is manifested in Jesus.[28]

[23] L. Cerfaux, *The Church in the Theology of St. Paul* (New York, 1959), pp. 93–110.

[24] For eschatological interpretation see also the *Book of Jubilees,* 16:20; *Book of Henoch,* 10:12–14. For selected texts, see C. K. Barrett, *The New Testament Background: Selected Documents* (London, 1958).

[25] H. Rondet, *The Theology of Sin* (Notre Dame, Ind., 1960), p. 24.

[26] St. Gregory the Great, *Homilia 2 in Evangelia* (Roman Breviary for Quinquagesima Sunday).

[27] J. Coppens, "Le fils d'Homme Danielique et les Relectures de Dan. VII," in *Eph. Théo. Lov.,* 37 (January–April, 1961), 35–40.

[28] J. J. Von Allman, *Vocabulaire Biblique,* p. 222.

2. Christ's attitude toward sin and sinners is psychologically different, say, from that of St. John the Baptist. The Baptist's message was similar to that of the Old Testament prophets and in a sense a continuation of that same message. "Repent or be punished." Speaking to diverse segments of the Jewish population who came out to see him he says, "Brood of vipers! Who advised you to flee before the gathering storm of anger? Well, then, let your conduct show your change of heart! I tell you . . . the axe lies ready to strike at the root of the trees; any tree, therefore, that does not produce sound fruit is cut down and thrown into the fire" (Mt 3:7–10). In other words, John is still under the influence of the fearsome days of Yahweh's wrath which was to precede the day of God's judgment. This theme, of course, remains true even in the fulfillment of the Old Testament prophecies through Christianity. With Christ appears judgment for those who reject Him, and salvation, even here on earth, for those who accept Him.[29]

Christ, in His preaching to the Jews, emphasizes a different aspect of sin and the sinner. He does not, outside of rare occasions, attack it directly as does St. John the Baptist. Sin and sinners did not arouse in Christ the threats of punishment and divine wrath, but rather divine pity and compassion for the erring sheep, the dead son, the prodigal son, etc.[30] Throughout the Synoptic Gospels, Christ refers to Himself and His mission as the suffering servant of Isaia who patiently bears the sins of others in vicarious atonement. He sees sinners — and even pagans, a term which was almost synonymous with sin — as "the people who sit in darkness who have seen a light, and for those who sat in the region and shadow of death light had dawned" (Mt 4:16). His favorite subjects deal with sinners. He dines with sinners and is often seen with them. "I have come to call not the just but sinners," and again, "Those who are well have no

29 I. De la Potterie, "Le Péché c'est l'Iniquité," in Nou. Rev. Théo., 78 (September–October, 1956), 787.

30 J. Haas, Die Stellung Jesu Zu Sünde und Sünder nach den vier Evangelien, pp. 123–130.

need of the physician, but those who are sick."

Christ, however, is still conscious that men are sinners. His first words to the Jews at the beginning of His public ministry are ones of penance: "Do penance, for the kingdom of heaven is close at hand" (Mt 4:17). He even has some rather stern words to address to the Jews. "I assure you that in fact you will, every one of you, likewise perish if you do not mend your evil ways" (Lk 13:5 [Conf. tr.]). But even here, the central theme of Christ's message is repentance out of love: the Father who welcomes the lost son with an embrace of love; a lost sheep who is joyously brought back to the flock on the shoulders of the pastor; a lost drachma which the owner spared no pain to find, etc. "I tell you, there is joy in heaven over one repentant sinner — more, in fact, than over ninety-nine saints that have no need of repentance" (Lk 15:7).

3. Another theme is introduced into the notion of sin through Christ's message. Christ offers salvation to those who accept Him, but also condemnation to those who reject Him. This condemnatory theme emerges and grows steadily with Israel's rejection of Him during His public life.[31] The culmination of this aspect comes when Israel rejects Christ totally in the passion and crucifixion. This will be the supreme sin for which there can be no forgiveness in this world or in the next because it is a rejection of the source of truth and light:

> Alas! This babe is destined
> to be the downfall no less
> than the restoration of many in Israel (Lk 2:34).

The theme of the rejection of Christ, as the Jews of old had rejected all the prophets, becomes a favorite theme in the early preaching or kerygma of the Apostles. "Blessed are you when men reproach you . . . for so did they persecute the prophets who were before you" (Mt 5:11 [Conf. tr.]). The miracles themselves become a stumbling block for some and an indication of

---

[31] A. Descamps, "Le Péché dans le Nouveau Testament," in *Théologie du Péché*, pp. 68–69.

God's presence for others. After Jesus cured the supplicant's withered hand in the temple (once again a sign for the Jews that Christ had also cured his sins) St. Matthew tells us that "the Pharisees walked out and resolved to put him out of the way" (Mt 12:14). Immediately following this passage which hints at the future destruction of Christ, the evangelist saw fit to quote the appropriate passage of the suffering servant of Yahweh (5:18–21). In other words, from here on, Christ begins His "mounting to Jerusalem" and to His expiatory death for sin and sinners. The death and resurrection become the images for the expiation of sin (to be further developed in the thought of St. Paul). But the presence of Christ in Jerusalem and the continued and bitter opposition of the Jews makes the crucifixion inevitable.[32] Christ died for sin and that He should so die seemed scandalous, but the seeming scandal is lessened, as it were, because it was so told in Holy Scripture. "This," he said to them, "is the gist of the Scriptures: the messias must suffer and on the third day rise from the dead. Furthermore: in his name the need of a change of heart and forgiveness of sins must be preached to all the nations . . ." (Lk 24:46–47). Thus the two themes of death and expiation of sin are closely united in these pericopes.

4. The above theme develops into the ecclesial discourses and parables and its presence among sinful members, within as well as without the Kingdom, becomes the Church in the world.[33] Within her there will always be the tension of sinful members mainly because the time between the beginning of the Kingdom and its consummation at the Parousia is the time of divine mercy, compassion, and forgiveness. Thus Christ presses the Apostles to work hard and unfailingly because "The harvest is ripe but the laborers are few." But the Kingdom remains full of sinners;

---

[32] F. X. Durwell, *The Resurrection: A Biblical Study* (New York, 1960), p. 27; H. Rondet, op. cit., pp. 32–33; A. Descamps, art. cit., *Théologie* . . . , pp. 73–76; A. Descamps, *Les Justes et la Justice* . . . , pp. 187–198.

[33] For explanation of this word in the Synoptic Gospels see R. Bultmann, *Theology of the New Testament*, Vol. I (London, 1956), pp. 254–259.

the Church in the world will always be a mixture of the good
and bad. See the series of parables explaining this theme in
the thirteenth chapter of St. Matthew's Gospel: the good and bad
seed must be allowed to grow until the harvest time (5–24).
Christ Himself gives the eschatological interpretation in verses
37–52; the net will gather all kinds of fishes but the good will
be separated from the bad only at night, etc. It is precisely in
this ecclesial[34] context that the leaders of the Kingdom (St. Peter
and the Apostles) are given the powers to forgive sin. This is in
both an ecclesial and an eschatological context since to forgive
sin is an anticipation of the final judgment, for "whatever you
shall loose on earth shall be loosed in heaven." The forgiveness
of sin is guaranteed precisely because it is an anticipation of the
final judgment[35] (Mt 17:17 and parallel passages). Thus the
Church is charged by Christ to continue the forgiveness of sin
on earth.

The forgiveness of sin is given to the Church but in a context
which proceeds from the expiatory value of Christ on the cross.
The death of Christ has eschatological value since sin is con-
quered by His death. The battle between Christ (and, now, His
Church) is to continue to the end of time (the net, the bad seed,
etc.), but the devil and sin are wounded mortally in and through
the death of Christ.[36]

5. One last remark on the messages of Christ in regard to
mutual charity and the forgiveness of sins. This aspect was mentioned in the preliminary remarks to this chapter, but it will be
worth the trouble to examine this important element more in
detail. Christ sums up all of the law — all justice to use the term
of St. Matthew — in the dual command of the love of God and
the love of neighbor (Mt 22:34; Lk 10:29). The true disciples of
Christ will be distinguished from sinners by the love they exercise
one for another. One's neighbor is anyone in need, and is not to

---

[34] We use this word to distinguish it from the word "ecclesiastical" which
has too much of a clerical ring to it. For further information in this regard,
see H. De Lubac, *The Splendour of the Church* (New York, 1957), p. 10.
[35] A. Lefevre, art. cit., *La Maison Dieu* . . . , p. 16.
[36] L. Cerfaux, *Christ in the Theology of St. Paul*, p. 114.

be restricted to persons of the same national origin or clan.[37] In spite of the many sins of the truly repentant sinner, his deep love disposes him for God's mercy more than any other element. "Therefore I tell you, her sins, which are many, are forgiven, for she loves much" (Lk 7:47 [Conf. tr.]). The bond of relationship is so strong in mutual love, forgiveness, etc., that it is as if the Christian does it to Christ Himself (Mt. 25:31). Love of one another is proposed as the principal deterrent and antidote to any and all sin; so much so that God's forgiveness of our sins is dependent upon the mutual forgiveness we have one for another.[38] Christ considered this mutual forgiveness as one of the greatest manifestations of mutual charity (Mt 6:14; 18:21; Lk 17:3; 23:24).

Conclusion. For the Christian, Christ is the friend of sinners (Mt 9:9–13; Mk 2:14) and is moved with compassion for them. This will take Him to the heights of His humiliating death for their salvation and forgiveness. This fundamental attitude is now left to the Kingdom on earth, the Church, which has the power to forgive sin in His name as an anticipation of His second coming.

This attitude is in contrast with that of the pharisees, this "perverse generation" that commits the greatest of all possible sins — rejecting Christ — which makes the forgiveness of their sins impossible (Mt 21:28, 33; 22:1–10; Lk 13:3; Mk 8:38). They do not possess the fundamental humility, which even the publicans and women of ill repute have, to recognize their sinful condition. As a result, the publicans and prostitutes will precede the pharisees into the Kingdom of heaven (Lk 18:9–14; 19:1–10; Mt 21:28–32). Ultimately, the publican and prostitute, by their humility, become the true clients and servants of God. The greatest obstacle to the Kingdom of God is not so much the number of sins themselves (although, certainly, this is very serious) but confidence in oneself and in one's own forces. Such an attitude makes even God's omnipotent mercy go for nothing.[39]

---

[37] R. Schnackenburg, Die Sittliche Botschaft, pp. 56–60.
[38] A. Descamps, "Le Jugement des Chrétiens d'Après Mt. 25:31," in Revue Diocesaine de Tournai, 6 (August, 1951), pp. 506–509.
[39] J. Dupont, Les Béatitudes (Louvain, 1960), p. 67.

III. Sin in the Theology of St. Paul

1. The theology of sin in the Epistles of St. Paul is one of the deepest developments in the thought of the Apostle of the Gentiles. The traditions of the Christian community were certainly his because he himself had to learn this primitive catechesis from the community itself. This is expressed in the early Epistles of the Apostle, particularly the two earliest to the Thessalonians.[40] We shall not attempt to divide the progressive thought of the Apostle on the notion of sin; it is sufficient to say that such a progress exists and if a complete picture of Paul's theology is desired, it will have to be considered in a more expanded study, which is not possible at this time. In this study only the general themes of St. Paul's thought on sin and its relationship in and through the death and the resurrection of Christ are explicated. No attempt will be made to give a detailed study of the idea of original sin in St. Paul, which would take us far beyond the scope of this limited chapter.[41] But what is essential in the great triumph of Christ (and in Him, Christians) over sin and death (which is the result of sin) is the death and the resurrection of Christ. This is central in Paul's thought. "The resurrection of Jesus attests to the triumph of the living God over the diabolical powers . . . it is the testimony of divine justice which offers salvation to sinners."[42] The death of sin is brought about only in Christ's death and resurrection; the only way the Christian can hope to participate in this salvific power of Christ is by mysteriously, yet really, undergoing this same death and resurrection in his own life. Nor can the resurrection be separated from this victory over sin; both death and resurrection form two parts of the same reality: death to sin and life in Christ (justification for St. Paul[43]). In the now famous words of

---

[40] L. Cerfaux, Christ . . . , pp. 3–6.

[41] Ch. Boyer, "Le Péché Originel," in Théologie du Péché, pp. 243–291.

[42] R. M. Achard, De la Mort à la Resurrection d'Après l'Ancien Testament (Geneva, 1955), p. 180; F. X. Durwell, op. cit., pp. 28–39.

[43] E. Tobac, Le Problème de la Justification d'Après St. Paul (Gembloux, 1941), pp. 58–65.

Father Durwell, who only repeats tradition, "Sin is expiated by death, but justice is only conferred following on the resurrection."[44] This death and resurrection are united, then, in the one act of baptism in which death and life are symbolically portrayed in the burying and rising from the waters (Rom 4:25). St. Paul teaches that although Christ's death has expiated our sins, our justification, which consists in the remission of our sins and the new life, is given to us only in the risen Christ. Man dies to sin and rises again to life in Christ (see the themes of death and life in Col 2:11; Rom 6:11; 8:2). In other words, for St. Paul sin takes on its full dimension only in the light of the Paschal mystery.[45]

2. The theme of God's wrath (which is the other side of His mercy and goodness) is well developed in the theology of St. Paul. What provokes this anger and wrath is the voluntary and inexcusable sins of men. This is the major theme of Rom 1:18–31: "The wrath of God is being revealed from heaven against all ungodliness and wickedness of those men who in wickedness stifle the truth of God." We have already pointed out that these phrases — wrath, justification, forgiveness of sin — all have a fundamentally eschatological meaning. This wrath of God is now an anticipation of the final judgment — even a beginning here below of that judgment. This theme was also quite popular in Jewish apocalyptical literature.[46] These sins are generators not only of death but also of visible and external effects such as wars, famine, and, as in our present text, base immorality of the worst kind. Sin is a kind of *lex talonis* in which the sinner pays for his sin by a like destruction of the goods and use of his own body. Thus sin (of the pagan world) was a voluntary ignorance of God and from this has issued immorality destroying the men it has inflicted. God has delivered them to impurity which dishonors the body just as these wicked men have corrupted the

---

[44] F. X. Durwell, *op. cit.*, p. 27.

[45] P. Anciaux, *op. cit.*, p. 16.

[46] A. Descamps, "L'Erreur Religieuse et Immoralité d'Après Romains I, 18–32," in *Revue Diocesaine de Tournai*, 6 (1951), pp. 22–30.

truth of God.[47] This biblical notion of self-destruction of man as soon as he has destroyed his relationship with God is as true today as it was then. It remains true, moreover, that for St. Paul, wars, famine, and the like are the results, in some mysterious way, of men's voluntary sins. It is interesting to note the list of sins that St. Paul enumerates in the first chapter of his Epistle to the Romans. Here he speaks of a "people without mercy," a very expressive term which characterizes the hardness of ancient civilizations and, in a very true sense, of all societies without God. Sin, then, for St. Paul produces its own destruction in the sinner who has committed it. Once man has abandoned God, God leaves man and is vowed to destruction (the wrath of God).

3. But how did Christ really overcome sin? That Christ overcame and expiated sin by His death and resurrection was a fundamental point in the soteriology of St. Paul. This was the victory of Christ over sin. The death of Christ for St. Paul is fundamental. "Jesus is the instrument of expiation in His blood: by His bloody cross, He has expiated for our sins and has reconciled us to God. The value of the sacrifice of the Cross resides acquired and active in the glorified Christ and it is this treasury of expiation that man must acquire for himself by faith; in giving himself to Christ, man makes his own the expiation which Christ has offered for us. It is thus that the sinner becomes just, the sinner a son."[48]

This whole aspect of death, sin, and expiation is well developed in Rom 3:23–26. "The insistence with which Paul comes back to the expiatory value of blood is easy to understand if he puts the death of Christ in the category of sacrifice, and compares it to those of the Old Testament."[49] It is thus that baptism and the death of Christ are linked by the same formula: the remission of sins. The confession of faith accompanying the sacra-

---

[47] L. Cerfaux, *Une Lecture* . . . , p. 27.

[48] J. Huby and S. Lyonnet, *Saint Paul: Epître aux Romains* (Paris, 1958), p. 155.

[49] L. Cerfaux, *Christ* . . . , p. 146. See also C. Spicq, *Agapè*, III (Paris, 1959), pp. 15–44.

ment always placed baptism in the context of death as an atonement (in this same vein see 1 Cor 15:3).

Paul, therefore, conceives of sin as a sort of state to which man is inextricably united. It is a manner of being in which the sinner finds himself. Hence, those who wished to save themselves from this terrible state had to unite themselves by faith to the crucified Christ. This incorporation of the sinner into the death (negative aspect) and the resurrection (positive element) of Christ is an ontological reality in which the sinner is radically transformed from the state of sinfulness to the state of justice, or God's own being in Christ. The relationship of the two terms demands the reality of both or the relationship is completely destroyed. But how, once again, did Christ do this? Paul's explanation is given in Rom 8:3 and Gal 3:13. In both these texts it is the body of Christ which repairs the offense by becoming, as it were, the object of the wrath of God. "The Incarnation consisted in taking 'sinful flesh,' which was exactly like that of sinners, and bringing all sinful flesh together in it. It was the condition for the condemnation of sin being fulfilled in the flesh of Christ and the way to life being opened up."[50] For St. Paul to picture this freedom from the state of sin, he had only to go to the common image of slavery then prevalent everywhere in the Roman Empire. We may also appeal to the Old Testament as a locus for this image of St. Paul. In these places, God freed His people from slavery as typified in the delivery from the slavery of Egypt (Dt 7:8; 9:26; 13:6; Neh 1:10; see passages in Rom 6:18; 20:22; 1 Cor 6:20; Gal 3:13). In delivering Himself to the cross, Christ killed sin in His body.[51]

4. It remains only to consider in some detail what St. Paul thinks of the relationship of the Christian to sin. Paul is very realistic and concrete in this regard. For the Christian to sin is to take the very members of Christ's body and to sin with them, so close is the relationship of Christ with Christians. "Do you not know that your bodies are members of Christ?

---

[50] *Ibid.*, p. 163.
[51] A. Descamps, *art. cit.*, *Théologie* . . . , p. 111.

Shall I therefore take the members of Christ and make them members of a prostitute? Never!" (1 Cor 6:15.) This is a very realistic picture. St. Paul uses no metaphor. For a Christian to sin is to use the members of Christ for an evil thing, a true sacrilege. We must realize that this context is so outspokenly realistic that to bring in any idea of a "mystical" body as distinct from a real body would be unfaithful to Paul's reasoning. The union of a physical body with another physical body is in question in the mention of intercourse with a prostitute, and to this St. Paul opposes union with the body of Christ as an antithesis. Realism of the relationships is therefore presupposed if we are to have any valid relationship.[52] By sinning in this way, the Christian desecrates the very body of Christ in some real but mysterious way.

We have already seen the contrast of diverse states of the sinner (state or being of sin and death), and that of the Christian (state or being of life in Christ). This antithesis is clearly brought out when Paul compares the work of Adam and Christ. Adam is a type of Christ. As a matter of fact, Adam was made in function of Christ and not vice versa. The sin of Adam, therefore, plunged all men into the state of spiritual death as well as physical death (which is the consequence of sin itself). The second element in the antithesis is the salvation brought in Christ over sin. The fall, therefore, is modeled on the plan of salvation. "For if by the offense of the one the many died, much more has the grace of God, and the gift which consists in the grace of the one man, Jesus Christ, overflowed into the many . . . the greater the offense became, so much the more has grace increased" (Rom 5:15–16, 20). This is also the parallel we find in the distinction between the "body of sin" and the "body of the spirit" mentioned so often in St. Paul (Rom 6:6; 7:24).[53]

The Christian is forever dead to sin. He has died once and for all in the saving waters of baptism which mystically obtained for

[52] L. Cerfaux, *The Church* . . . , p. 280.
[53] H. Rondet, *op. cit.*, p. 40.

him the saving powers of Christ's death and resurrection (Rom 6:10–11). The image is clearly presented to us as an ontological reality, not as some fictitious atoning for men by Christ. Once again, it is the entrance of the celestial life into the terrestrial.

From all this there follow some important consequences for the Christian. His actions must follow his being; he must act as a son of light and not of darkness (sin). To be holy, to keep God's laws and commandments is a very grave moral obligation incumbent on every Christian.[54] The diverse moral prescriptions are but the occasion for the Christian to prove his love for God. The law for him has now become not a subject of death, but an additional proof of God's love.[55]

But there still exists a tension. The Christian has not as yet arrived at his final goal. He must be watchful and "mortify his members which are on earth" (Col 2:18). The regenerated man is still weak (Gal 5:17). He is not safe from the seductions of concupiscence (Rom 8:13). Man, even regenerated, can violate the temple of God (1 Cor 3:17), and he can crucify once again the Christ who lives in him (Heb 6:6) and thus expel the Spirit (1 Thes 5:19). The Christian must work out his salvation in "fear and trembling."

CONCLUSION

The salvific justice of God is manifested both in His wrath and in His salvation in Christ. Christ has expiated the sins of men and has therefore reconciled all men with God. He offers man the way to maintain this intimate and personal relationship with God. Humanity is justified in Him and possesses the force, in communion with the Spirit of Christ, to conquer the tyranny of sin. The new humanity, of which Christ is the principle, is

[54] B. Rigaux, *Epîtres aux Thess.* (Paris, 1958), pp. 489–492.
[55] S. Lyonnet, "Liberté Chrétienne et la Loi de l'Esprit," in *Christus: Cahiers Spirituels*, 1954, no. 4, pp. 16–20.

formed and redeemed from sin by faith and baptism which reproduces in man the death and resurrection of Christ. The Christian is forever dead to sin, incorporated as he is into Christ where he receives the divine pardon for his sins, divine justice, and the liberating Spirit. To live the life of Christ "who loved me and sacrificed himself for me" (Gal 2:20) is to renounce the reality and the state of sin forever.

CHAPTER IV

Theological Reflections and Effects of Sin

INTRODUCTION

Even though Dostoevsky never intended *The Brothers Karamazov* to be a theological treatise, his main idea that "hell is nothing else than the suffering of those who are incapable of love" reveals with true Christian and theological profundity what sin actually is. In another passage in the same work the author has one of his characters say: "I feel that we are all patricides. We have all helped to assassinate the father who is in us and thus there is no son who has not killed his own father." Such a distant figure as Origen said the same thing: "*ubi peccata, ibi multitudo, ibi schismata, ibi dissensiones, ibi divisio.*"[1] The basis of the theology of this ancient Christian author was that man was made in God's image and likeness, and that sin entered into man's life only to disfigure and destroy that image. The redemptive work of Christ serves to restore that filial image by the destruction of sin.[2]

If the essence of sin in Christianity is the destruction of the relationship between two persons, God and man, it is also the destruction of the social relationship which exists between Chris-

---

[1] Origen, *In Ezech.*, hom. 9, n. 1. See H. De Lubac, *Catholicism* (London, 1955), pp. 6–15; K. Barth on the threefold opposition caused by sin: "opposition to God, to oneself and to one's neighbor," "l'Eglise et les Eglises," in *Oecumenica*, 14 (1936), 139. See also the many patristic texts cited in the work of De Lubac, pp. 14–16.

[2] "All that we do in each hour, in each moment impresses an image on us. Therefore, we ought to examine each of our acts one by one, to examine our motives for each act and each word, to see if it is a celestial image or a terrestrial one which is imprinted in our souls," *Hom. in Ps.*, 38, II, 2 (*P.G.*, XII, col. 1403D f.). For this whole doctrine see H. Crouzel, *Théologie de l'Image de Dieu Chez Origène* (Paris, 1956), pp. 181–215.

tians themselves. Man is social in nature, a solidarity in the Mystical Body of God in good and in evil. If one is hurt, all are hurt, if one does good, the same good redounds to the benefit of the whole ecclesial organism.[3] Every sin, then, destroys this relationship between Christian and Christian. The one who offends becomes debtor to him against whom he has sinned — in this case, all Christians — and the one sinned against becomes obligated to forgive and to pray for the return of the errant member of the one Body of Christ. St. Augustine mentions this aspect repeatedly. For, he says, we are not making a fictitious petition when we confess each day to God, to all the saints, "and to you, brothers," that we have sinned against them all; so, too, in our asking for forgiveness in the second part of the same *Confiteor* we ask and entreat our brothers to pray for us to God for forgiveness: "and you, brothers, pray for me to the Lord our God."[4] Therefore sin can never be considered as a purely individual affair in Christianity. One has sinned against God, above all, and the Body of Christ, the Church; the sinner must make reparation to both.[5] Trotsky saw just the antithesis of this attitude when he said, "Lenin and I turned to Christianity to seek a solution for the diverse evils of humanity: but we found only a prophylactic of individual salvation, an art of abstaining from sin." This aspect shall be examined in more detail later.

Christianity has distinguished between the diverse degrees and categories of sin. It became necessary in the course of time to make a distinction between mortal and venial sin because of

---

[3] "There is a brotherhood of common responses: they answer the same appeal and enjoy the same communion in the same love; it is as if one and the same blood flowed in their veins," H. De Lubac, *The Splendour of the Church* (New York, 1956), p. 32; see also Y. Congar, *The Mystery of the Church* (Baltimore, 1960), p. 127; A. Plé, "The Virtue of Love," in *Love of Our Neighbor* (Springfield, Ill., 1955), p. 78; P. Charles, "L'Esprit Catholique," in *L'Eglise Sacrement du Monde* (Tournai, 1960), pp. 136–137.

[4] J. Leclercq, "Le Sainté Église et la Rémission des Péchés," in *L'Eglise et le Pecheur* (Paris, 1941), p. 22; A. Smoeck, *Confession and Pastoral Psychology* (Westminster, Md., 1960), pp. 50–74.

[5] R. Blome, "Les Dimensions du Péché," in *Coll. Mech.*, 30 (1930), pp. 571–579.

the results of sin and its consequent punishment.[6] The foundation for this classification lies in the irreparable or reparable
character of the resultant condition of sin. These notions shall
also be investigated later.[7]

In a text that was attributed to St. Augustine, but which
probably does not belong to him, we read the following touching
story:

> Mary and Martha and the crowd who followed them shed tears
> of supplication for the deceased. The Church asks God to have
> mercy on him. The sinner must make a strong effort to remain
> and to stay within the Church: if the unity of the Church does
> not come to his aid and if she does not intercede for what he
> cannot hope to receive, the soul of the deceased will not be
> snatched from the hands of its enemy. We must believe, there-
> fore, that all the sacrifices of the entire Church, all the prayers,
> good works help him who, to convert himself, begins by recogniz-
> ing that he is dead to grace. Thus no one can perform worthy
> penance who is not aided by the unity of the Church. . . . He
> who separates himself from the Church loses the benefit thereof
> and how can he perform efficacious penance unless he regains the
> unity and goodness of Holy Mother the Church? How can he hope
> to find God well disposed in his regard, he who has not feared
> to offend her who is His most holy spouse, His Mother, His
> daughter and sister and whose aid the sinner has despised?[8]

The theological notions of the effects of sin (venial — mortal)
and its essential ecclesial character will be combined along the
pattern suggested by St. Augustine. Participation in the divine
life can be fully received and lived only in the living community of the faithful which is the Church. The grace of Christianity is essentially a fraternal grace because it makes us sons
of God in Christ. That is why in the Christian perspective
sin has essentially an ecclesial signification. "Mortal" sin is a
breaking-off with God as well as a deprivation of divine grace;

---

[6] P. Anciaux, *Le Sacrément de la Pénitence* (Louvain, 1960), pp. 36–37.

[7] P. Anciaux, *op. cit.*, p. 50; K. Rahner, "Vergessene Wahrheiten über
das Bussakrament," in *Geist und Leben*, 30 (1953), 340–343; D. Braun,
"Dogmatische Beschouwingen over de Biecht," in *Ned. Kath. Stemmen.*,
14 (1957), 84–95.

[8] *De Vera et Falsa Poenitentia*, XI–XII (P.L., 40, 1123). See also the
Decretum Gratiani, De Poenitentia, d. VI, C. 1.

it is, by that very fact, a crime and a "mortal" blow against the community of God. Venial sin is also an attack on the community, against the bonds of love which unite the whole community in one body. It diminishes the vital forces in one of the members of this community. It means a diminution in the capacity of love. It is only in this light that we shall understand the full theological implications of the notion of sin.[9]

I. Mortal and Venial Sin

Perhaps the most Christian as well as theological notion of sin signifies contradiction of the divine will, disobedience to it, apostasy from it. By its essence and by its effects, sin is a negation of Christian perfection and a renunciation of the following of Christ.[10] In the final analysis, sin is a refusal to love God and neighbor. It is a profound egoism which is expressed in a basic insubordination to God's law (a transgression) and an inordinate attachment to one's own will in placing one's end in a creature or created reality. The traditional definition of sin as a turning from God and conversion to creatures is, therefore, clearly justified.[11]

But not all sins are of the same gravity and seriousness. Scripture and Tradition, as well as the Church, have always maintained the distinction between grave or mortal sins (*peccata criminalia, capitalia*) and venial sin (*peccata levia, venialia, quotidiana*). There are many references in Scripture to diverse categories which beget death and others which exclude one from the Kingdom of God (Rom 6:23; 5:16; Gal 5:19; 1 Cor 6:9). Although the terms "mortal" sin and "venial" sin are not found in Scripture as such, the reality is nevertheless there. The Fathers of the Church unanimously testify that slight faults, for

---

[9] See Th. Deman in article "Le Péché," in *Dict. Theo. Cath.*, XII, Col. 226; St. Thomas, *Summa Theologiae*, I, II, q. 88, art. 2; I, II, q. 87, a. 6; I, II, q. 73, art. 3; *De Malo* II, a. 10.

[10] F. Tillemann, *The Master Calls* (Baltimore, 1960), p. 70.

[11] B. Häring, *The Law of Christ*, I (Westminster, Md., 1960), p. 354; J. Leclercq, *Christians in the World* (New York, 1961), pp. 75–122.

instance, do not entail the loss of grace. It is mostly to St. Augustine that we owe the clearer precision and clarification of the doctrine of the essential distinction between venial and mortal sin.[12] Similarly, the Council of Carthage expressly taught that every just man, even the saint, correctly and justly prays for himself: "forgive us our trespasses."[13] The Council of Trent took care to note that there are sins which do not destroy the state of grace.[14]

But in what exactly does the distinction between mortal and venial sin reside? Fundamentally, it rests on the irreparable character *in se* of the state of mortal sin and its consequent eternal punishment. Sin can be compared to the state of sickness of the human body: if it attacks the vital functions of the organism, it is said to be mortal or deadly; but if it simply weakens the diverse forces of that body, it is not so serious or dangerous; it is, in such a case, not mortal or deadly. So, too, in the supernatural sphere. Mortal sin "constitutes a true separation from God which is *in se* irreparable by only human forces."[15] While it remains true that in Christian theology this "death" is definitive only after physical death and that while yet living a man can be converted from his sinful state, still, in itself, the state of mortal sin is such that outside of God's grace and mercy, nothing could ever repair it. "The healing of our sickness," remarks St. Thomas,

> comes to us either inwardly from ourselves or both inwardly from ourselves and from outside ourselves at the same time. Thus, when a man has a light sickness, he can cure himself by the sole forces of his healthy constitution. But if the sickness is more serious, he must have the services of a doctor. However, one cannot imagine a case in which the medication alone would bring about our healing since in the final analysis man has in himself the principle of life thanks to which he can recover his health.[16]

---

[12] *De Civ. Dei*, XXI, C. 27, 5 (*P.L.*, XLI, c. 750).

[13] D.B. 106, 107.

[14] D.B. 804. "Licet enim in hac mortali vita quantumvis sancti et justi in levia saltem et quotidiana, quae etiam venialia dicuntur, peccata quandoque cadant non propterea desinunt esse justi."

[15] P. Anciaux, *op. cit.*, p. 38.

[16] *De Malo*, q. 2, a. 10.

In other words, the state of mortal sin is compared to a deadly disease in which the help of a doctor (God) is absolutely necessary. Even in this case, however, God cannot cure the sinner alone; even God must have at least the good will and help of the sick man. St. Thomas is simply repeating the Augustinian adage: "God has created you without you; He will not save you without you." In this light, then, venial sin does not attack or destroy the essential relationships between God and man; it does not bring about spiritual death. Venial sins are negligences, the lack and weakness of complete love given to the Creator; they are a lack of fervor and a sign of lukewarmness. They signify a slowing down or a detour in the progress of the Christian toward perfection.[17]

Even in the case of irreparable sins there are different degrees. In most mortal sins, the virtues of faith and hope remain.[18] Should it happen that the sinner sin even against these two virtues, there still remains the baptismal character and, hence, a radical capacity for the reception of sanctifying grace. We must qualify the notion of mortal sin as a "death" or "irreparable loss." Mortal sin results in the destruction of the life of God in a man; in a very true sense, he is dead to God. But on the other hand, he retains a radical capacity, as long as life still continues on earth, for conversion and divine life. From this point of view, we must call the state of mortal sin a grave sickness for the sinner. Insofar as the "irreparable loss" of this state is concerned, St. Thomas says:

> For sin, being a sickness of the soul, is said to be mortal in comparison with a disease, which is said to be mortal, through causing an irreparable defect consisting in the corruption of a principle. Now the principle of the spiritual life, which is a life in accord with virtue, is the order to the last end; and if this order be corrupted, it cannot be repaired by any intrinsic princi-

---

[17] G. Thils, *Sainteté Chrétienne* (Tielt, 1958), pp. 493–495; P. De-Letterer, "Venial Sin and its Final Goal," in *The Thomist*, 18 (1953), 32–70. English trans. of Thils, *Christian Holiness* (Tielt, 1961).

[18] V. Vergriete, "Sin," in *Man and His Happiness*, Vol. III in *Theological Library* (Chicago, 1957), p. 238.

ple. . . . Wherefore such sins are called mortal as being irreparable.
. . . Accordingly, mortal and venial are opposed as reparable and
irreparable: and I say this with reference to the intrinsic principle,
but not to the Divine Power, which can repair all diseases, whether
of body or of soul.[19]

Even within each of these categories of sin, however, there
are degrees of gravity, and so sin must be measured more accu-
rately than by a simple division into mortal and venial. This
rather simple division of the diverse nature of sin has been
criticized by some theologians. "Our Christian people need to be
enlightened on this point. There is too great a tendency among
them not to make any comparison of sins except between mortal
and venial, a distinction based on the effects of sin. They are
inclined to think that on either side of this line of demarcation
sins are equal."[20] Or again, in the words of another famous theologian, "Mortal and venial sin qualify sin in regard to its effect
since it sometimes obliges a man to undergo temporal punishment and sometimes eternal. It is, however, very important not
to let this study get out of place and to develop it properly. In
many modern books of theology, this distinction has been given
a special place and this threatens the exactness of the notions."[21]

This distinction between mortal and venial sin ought to be
understood in the light of man's nature, for man is, by nature,
a being continuously perfecting himself (or destroying himself)
by the orientation of his acts. Modern psychology and psycho-
analysis have shown the importance of a "fundamental choice or
orientation" which gives significance and value to man's basic
existence. Reputable psychologists agree that neurosis and sometimes even cases of psychosis can be brought on by a lack of

---

[19] I, II, q. 88, art. 1.

[20] Vergriete, *op. cit.*, p. 238. See the words of Pius XII in his encyclical
Mystici Corporis Christi: "every sin, even grave sin, does not have as a result
to separate a man from the body of the Church — as would such sins as
schism, heresy and apostasy. All life does not disappear from those who, having
lost charity and sanctifying grace by sin, have become, as a consequence, incapable of supernatural merit, still conserve Christian faith and hope, and by
divine grace, under the interior inspirations of the Holy Spirit, are driven to
a salutary fear and urged on by God to prayer and penance for their sins."

[21] Th. Deman, "Le Péché," in *D.T.C.*, XII, col. 226.

significance and value to one's whole existence.[22] In other words,
the true meaning of the whole of human life, of each of our
actions, is founded on a profound orientation of our will, a
"choice which is fundamental" and which acts for each individual as a last end and overall meaning to his life. "Each man
chooses for himself a last end, a value to which he subordinates
all other values and in view of which he orients all his tendencies and his actions."[23] There are in each of us many tendencies
which are not naturally ordered, and it is only natural that these
diverse tendencies should conflict. They must, therefore, be integrated into a whole that conforms to some supreme value we
have chosen. This basic value or tendency is called our fundamental choice or orientation. A man can, for instance, choose a
monetary value as being supreme in his life. In that case, every
other value and action will be at the service of this one tendency; even the moral tendency to follow the will of God may
be directed to this end. Thus, God's will will be subordinate
to the pursuit of money, and if there should be a conflict between
the two, it will be resolved in favor of monetary values. In the
case of the fervent Christian, however, it is taken for granted
that his fundamental and basic value and "choice" in life is a
moral one, i.e., the will of God in all things.[24] He will, therefore,
bring all other values and tendencies to conform with this. Yet
man is limited in his judgment and his will is undermined by
his passions, habits, errors, etc. He performs actions which do
not serve this fundamental choice. They are, as it were, illogical
actions which can come upon the Christian through weakness
and malice.

If the Christian performs actions which are inconsistent but

[22] The very interesting studies of the famous Vienna psychologist, V.
Frankel in his works *The Doctor and the Soul* and *From a Death Camp
to Existentialism*.
[23] P. Anciaux, op. cit., p. 42.
[24] For a description of this moral tendency as forming man's supreme
value or choice see Max Scheler, *On the Eternal Man* (New York, 1961),
pp. 15–43; George Bull, "The Function of the Catholic College," in
Literature, the Channel of Culture (New York, 1948), pp. 22–23.

which, nevertheless, do not destroy his fundamental choice to do God's will, they are not strong enough to cause a break between God and himself. This we call venial sin. "Venial sin does not have the force of mortal sin. It does not include an undertaking as regards one's final end. For this reason, it does not attain the full definition of sin which includes opposition to the divine law. Venial sin does not separate us from God. It constitutes a disorder since man loves a creature outside of the divine order but it is not so strong as to cause a break. It is, so to speak, illogical on the sinner's part since he remains radically attached to God but nevertheless performs an act not directed towards him."[25]

There are actions, however, which are in flagrant opposition to the Christian's fundamental moral choice. He prefers the lower tendency to that which is supreme, the will of God. He therefore destroys the supreme relationship and reduces it to a lower end that serves his own egoism and self-satisfaction. In making God subservient to his own selfish ends, man has rejected God as God, for God can never be the means for man to attain an inferior good.

In the last analysis, the distinction between mortal and venial sin is based on a difference in the very nature of each of these faults. The quality or the seriousness of sin is determined either objectively or subjectively. The objective and proportional gravity of sin is objectively based on the hierarchy of values in relation to man's last end, which is God. Thus man's actions can be more or less grave, v.g., sins against God such as blasphemy. Less serious are sins of man against man, either against his physical or spiritual life. The less grave would be those against sub-human creatures, v.g., stealing, etc. In this category of objective sin, the action is judged in itself in relationship to man's last end. The whole purpose of moral theology is to discover and describe this fundamental hierarchy of values in relationship to the ultimate end of the Christian life. This science is obliged

---

[25] V. Vergriete, art. cit., in *Man* . . . , p. 263.

to elucidate and order these diverse obligations.[26]

In other words — still considering the objective criteria of sin — our union with God by charity is the Christian meaning of the human person. Consequently, sins directly against God are worse than sins directly against man. Those sins which are directly against man's internal goods (e.g., murder) are worse than those which attain only to his external goods (e.g., theft). In each of these sins, however, we must be very careful to note all the circumstances which can change or add a new moral implication to a particular act. Fornication, for instance, consists in having sexual relations with a person who is not one's spouse. If the circumstance is added that this person is married to another, the sin of injustice is committed in addition. This is what makes adultery a more serious sin than fornication.

Besides this fundamental objective criterion of sin, there is also the subjective element to consider. The gravity and culpability of an action will depend on the free will and deliberation of the subject. The internal relationship between the action and the last end established by the person who acts determines the degree of gravity of the sin. In other words, responsibility is present only insofar as an act is a human act. For example, a man can so intensely engage himself in a more or less insignificant action that he is guilty of mortal sin. Small as the action was in itself, it has become serious for him because he has made it a last end, a fundamental choice. Whatever tends to deter the will in its free movement (i.e., passion, violence, fear, etc.) diminishes, as a general rule, the culpability of the sinner. In extreme cases, moreover, a complete ignorance, a physical constraint to which no consent is given, certain pathological deficiencies which totally suppress voluntariness, suppress sin as well.

Determining the gravity of sin, St. Thomas strongly insists that the subjective element is most important and that a positive disposition is absolutely necessary. In the *Summa Theologiae*, I–II, questions 73, 77, and 78, St. Thomas compares spiritual

---

[26] Th. Deman, "Le Péché," in *DTC*, XII, col. 227–234; St. Thomas, *De Malo*, II, a. 10; *Summa Theologiae*, I, II, q. 73, a. 3.

with carnal sins. He explains that carnal sins are often less grave because they come from a profound weakness in man. On the other hand, spiritual sins are more deliberate since man has more control over his higher faculties. In both cases, the subjective elements are most important. In any case, any evaluation of such an internal disposition is a very difficult thing indeed. Most theologians counsel prudence when dealing with this matter. "At a certain point at least, determinations (of subjective guilt) are difficult and can only produce a quantity of opinions. We can even ask ourselves in what measure this audacious pursuit of the mortal and venial among the infinite details of human actions represents a real progress in moral theology. We explicitly call to mind these words of St. Augustine: 'What sins are venial, what mortal, must be judged by God, not by man' (*Enchiridion*, 78)."[27]

Yet, this simple distinction between mortal and venial sin can falsify our outlook. The Christian moral is positive, and in no way negative. In its essential form, it is simply the idea of following Christ.[28] In this fundamentally Christian conception of the moral life, the following and imitation of Christ, our goal ought to be a constant attempt to achieve more of God's love. As a matter of fact, "it does not suffice to say: he who does not advance, falls back. We must go further and better than this. The obligation to progress (in the spiritual life) is not only a sort of practical necessity for him who fears to backslide. It is a sort of radical necessity and a principle of the Christian life. To grow in Christ is an obligation which is always incumbent on every Christian. The fact of not wishing to progress is in itself a sin."[29] Therefore, in this context, venial sin is the greatest

---

[27] Th. Deman, *art. cit.*, DTC, XII, col. 226.

[28] F. Tillmann, *Die Idee der Nachfolge Christi*, Band III, pp. 9–14.

[29] Y. De Montcheuil, *Problèmes de Vie Spirituelle* (Paris, 1938), p. 66. In this same vein one may see an interesting note by Fr. Rondet in *The Theology of Sin*, p. 91: "We are familiar with the medieval principle: 'conscientia erronea ligat.' But it has sociological applications today. A collective conscience whose dictates seem to oblige the individual conscience interposes itself between the law, the remote rule of morality, and the individual conscience, which is the proximate norm. To reform the latter, it is often-

evil in the world after mortal sin and the Christian is always
under strict obligation to avoid even this. The "how far can I
go without committing a mortal sin" attitude betrays a vitiated
moral sense in any Christian. St. Thomas himself warns that it is
dangerous to commit venial sins since they incline us to mortal
sin. In any case, venial sin expresses a lukewarmness, a lack of
love which sooner or later will tell on exterior actions. It is a
mentality and a state unworthy of the fervent Christian.[30]

II. The Mentality of the Sinner

When dealing with what actually constitutes the nature or
definition of sin, there are usually three mentalities with which
the modern Christian is acquainted. Sin is either considered as
a disobedience, or as an interior disorder, or, finally, as a destruction of divine charity and a refusal to love.[31] Let us examine
each a little more in detail.

The first mentality sees sin essentially as a disobedience to
God's law or those of the Church. God gives a certain number
of precepts to which man is obliged to conform. If he does so,
he will, with God's grace, merit a right to an eternal reward —
heaven. Habitually, this forms the matter for any examination
of conscience before confession. In this conception, the adult
Christian is free to say yes or no to God. If he revolts, eternal
death in hell awaits him.

This rather simplified exposé of this particular mentality is
not to be lightly dismissed. The Old Testament as well as the
New speaks of obedience to God's law as a matter for life or
death (1 Jn 3:4).[32] The Book of Genesis puts this into clear

times necessary to reform the collective conscience of a milieu or of an
epoch."
  [30] J. Leclercq, *L'Enseignement de la Morale Chrétienne* (Paris, 1957),
pp. 4–23.
  [31] J. Regnier, *Le Sens du Péché* (Paris, 1954), pp. 26–48, English trans.
What Is Sin? (Westminster, Md., 1961); A. M. Roguet, *The Sacraments:
Signs of Life* (London, 1957), pp. 94–97; H. Rondet, *The Theology of Sin*
(Notre Dame, Ind., 1960), pp. 82–105.
  [32] J. Guellet, *Themes of the Bible* (Notre Dame, Ind., 1960), pp. 58–65.

terms: sin is a transgression of God's law which Adam committed, and because of this insubordination, Adam and his posterity must suffer and die. God is the supreme and ultimate criterion of His law: man must unflinchingly obey because He is God and for no other reason.[33]

While granting and keeping what is true in this conception of sin, we must conclude that, for the Christian, it is altogether insufficient. The fundamental drawback of this whole mentality is a lack of personal and integrated motivation for keeping God's law. To keep law for law's sake without a strong interior motivation (v.g., out of love and realization) is bordering on the infantile.[34] The law remains at all times, but as the Christian grows up spiritually, he recognizes the value intrinsic in the law to which he corresponds by personal acceptance and motivation.[35] Modern psychology has shown that command can be harmful to the adult who has no realization of its fundamental signification and meaning. This failure personally to justify and integrate even childhood commands is one of the main reasons for emotional disturbances in later adult life.[36]

A second serious objection is that this type of mentality restricts itself to the image of God as "lawmaker" whose commandments must be kept in fear and trembling. What then becomes of the Fatherhood of God so often and so insistently preached by Christ in practically all the pages of the New Testament?

Finally, this mentality produces a rather static idea of Christian moral and Christian perfection in general.[37] Its object becomes "What do I have to do?" or "How far can I go without committing serious sin?" By making God's laws simply external rules of morality and conduct, the Christian further leaves him-

---

[33] J. Regnier, *op. cit.*, pp. 28–29.
[34] A. Kriekemans, *Principes de l'Education Religieuse, Morale et Sociale* (Louvain, 1955), pp. 64–77.
[35] See this same principle applied so wonderfully in the little book of J. Mourrou, *The Act of Faith* (New York, 1959), pp. 6–18.
[36] J. Leclercq, *L'Enseignement . . .*, pp. 24–30.
[37] Ch. Boulanger, *La Doctrine Catholique*, t. IV, pp. 236–258.

self wide open to the baneful spirit of juridicism or legalism. "From the eighteenth century we have been submitted to diverse voluntarian notions of the law: law becomes the expression of a will, of a king or an assembly; to be moral, in consequence, is to act by respect of the law which is the final criterion of action. Theology swiftly became a catalogue of commandments and, along with it, Christian moral became the science of duties."[38] The danger of legalism has become more prevalent in our day. The conclusion to be drawn is that given this mentality, all that is not imposed by law belongs to the category of "superrogatory works" or even simply, "perfection." The study of moral theology becomes simply a study of sin and its limits, degrees, culpability, etc. In the words of Canon Leclercq: "One must have the courage to recognize that this morality . . . contrasts with the official teaching."[39] In the beginning of our moral life, therefore, we have need of commandments; it is by law and respect for authority that conscience and a sense of responsibility are formed and that we learn to recognize a sin as a sin. Yet, it is dangerous to assimilate a moral fault with an infraction of it. A command, which is very necessary in educating children, ought to give way little by little to motives of reason, to a personally justified system of values. In the words of St. Paul "the law must become an interiorized law."[40] To define evil exclusively by disobedience to a commandment is to give the appearance of liberty to revolt.[41]

The second frame of reference for sin is conceived of as a disorder of nature. This is aptly brought out by St. Thomas in the *Summa* (I–II, q. 93, a. 1). In such a conception, sin is

[38] G. Thils, *Sainteté* . . . , pp. 8–12; J. DeGuibert, *The Theology of the Spiritual Life* (New York, 1956), pp. 44–48.

[39] J. Leclercq, *op. cit.*, p. 11, as cited in J. Ford and G. Kelley, *Contemporary Moral Theology*, I (Westminster, Md., 1958), p. 52.

[40] On this important relationship between the law and Christian liberty, see S. Lyonnet, "Liberté Chrétienne et Loi de l'Esprit," in *Christus, Cahiers Spirituels*, 1954, no. 4, pp. 16–20.

[41] J. Regnier, *op. cit.*, p. 34; M. Huftier, "Péché Actuel," in *Théologie du Péché* (Tournai, 1960), pp. 340–344.

forbidden by God because it is a destruction of our spiritual being. Laws are not arbitrarily imposed on us by God, but are set up to function for our temporal and eternal good. God has created man according to a set pattern, in the compass of certain laws of being, which man must keep under pain of his own destruction or disintegration. Sin, above all, is a disintegrating factor because it destroys the order set up by God. In revolting against God, man has revolted against himself, and nature, in turn, has revolted against man. A whole chain of disorders is set up because of sin. Thus, obedient service to God is not a purely arbitrary or purely external law of our being; it comes from our very nature. Sin, therefore, becomes an obstacle to our perfection, to progressive realization of ourselves as men, for God has so ordained us that unless we submit to Him, we destroy and dismember ourselves. To sin is to destroy ourselves by going against the rule of good and evil, our reasonable nature as God has created it.[42]

This conception of moral law and sin is a vast improvement over the former mentality since there is a strong element of motivation and interiorization present. It even remains true that the struggle for good and the combat against evil is an element of integration and self-realization. Renouncement, mortification, and self-discipline take on positive notions in this context.[43]

Yet even here some observations are in order. There is a constant danger, in such a mentality, of losing the sense of God and degenerating into a pure humanism. I do not sin because by sinning I become less a man; I do treat or respect others as persons, not as things, because I too am a person. The "I — thou" relation becomes the fundamental relation. "I — thou —

---

[42] It is interesting to note that modern psychologists have also discovered this element of disintegration in the notion of moral evil. See the interesting symposium, *Conflict and Light* (New York, 1956), pp. 51–106, especially the articles by R. Allers and P. Cossa.

[43] P. Riga, "Penance, Mortification and Love," in *Cross and Crown*, 24 (Winter, 1961), 18–24.

God" can easily be abandoned in such a context.[44] It is a grave danger to forget that, in Christianity, the integration of man's nature is fundamentally the work of grace and not of renouncement and effort. God alone can lead this struggle to a successful end by giving His healing grace.[45] In this context, however, the law becomes the interior promptings of the Holy Spirit who leads us and speaks to us in law and objective commands. The law thus appears "as restoring the soul and rejoicing the very heart of man" (Ps 19).

The third mentality is perhaps the most perfect and the most Christian of all: to sin is a fundamental negation of charity, a refusal to love in return.[46] Man is made to love. As a matter of fact, man can be defined as the only animal in creation who is capable of disinterested love. And yet the paradox of love is that a man must give, and in proportion as he gives of himself, he both proves his love and fulfills his being. To refuse love, to refuse to give fully of ourselves is to destroy ourselves. We are thus released from the slavery of law and obligation and brought into the realm of Christian freedom; obligation and commandment remain, to be sure, but its spirit is radically different from that of the slave who does not see the intrinsic reason in love of the law:

> Having once known what it is to be loved freely, one no longer finds any flavor in submissions.
> When one has known what it means to be loved by free men, the prostrations of slaves no longer please.[47]

In such a context, the danger of egoism is radically eliminated, for one does not live for oneself but for others. "To be a person is to respond to the love which called me first."[48] St. Thomas

---

[44] A. Dondeyne, "Existential Phenomenology: Credit and Debit," in *Contemporary European Thought and Christian Faith* (Pittsburgh, 1958), pp. 108–122.

[45] St. Thomas, *Summa Theologiae*, I, II, q. 106, a. 1.

[46] B. Häring, *The Law of Christ*, I, pp. 63–64; H. Rondet, op. cit., pp. 83–84.

[47] Charles Peguy, *God Speaks* (New York, 1957), p. 42.

[48] J. Lacroix, *Vocation Personelle et Tradition Nationale*, p. 188.

teaches the same doctrine: "The good of virtue is the ordering of love" (*De Malo*, II, 10).

In being raised to the dignity of a son of God, man is thereby raised to an undreamed-of spiritual level. Love has become charity and consequently "all the moral and religious obligations, the essentials of the Kingdom of God, can be reduced to love."[49] Charity is spread in our hearts by the Holy Spirit (Rom. 5:6). To respond to this love is the essential obligation of the Christian. It cannot be a matter of simple formalism or external conformity to a law. It must be a full and total giving of oneself both to God and to neighbor in unity with the one Mystical Body of Christ. To sin is to refuse to correspond to this love of God, to destroy the relationship of love between two lovers. And that is not all. Refusal to love obstructs the growth of the whole of the Mystical Body; it harms the neighbor as well as the individual himself. It is a separation from God, our Father, and our brethren in Christ. This is probably the profoundest Christian conception of sin, and for the Christian, hell "can only be the suffering of those who cannot love." Not to love, or to refuse to love, is the greatest evil imaginable in Christianity. In this context, sin is seen for what it is: a refusal of communion in love with God and the neighbor.

III. THE SOCIAL ASPECT OF SIN

This element of the personal offense by any and every sin against all the brethren in the Mystical Body of Christ deserves some further treatment. As we have said, sin has fundamentally a threefold dimension: It is primarily an offense against God, our Father, whose love we have rejected; it is a destruction of our sonship since we have refused the condition on which our sonship is based — a loving and obedient return of that love; and lastly, it is an offense against all the members of the Mystical Body. The first two dimensions of sin are easily understood, but the third remains a mystery to most Christians. How

---

[49] J. Bonsriven, *Les Enseignements de Jesus-Christ* (Paris, 1952), p. 125.

can my sin, personal and sometimes secret as it is, offend every other member of the Body of Christ?

The ecclesiological revival of our day has stressed the notion of the Mystical Body of Christ; it is the unique means of salvation in whose sphere alone the Holy Spirit vivifies and raises up saints conformed to the image of the Son of God.[50] ". . . The early Christian did not believe that he could have access to God apart from the community. But for him the community was the new people of God, the body of Christ which is the Church."[51] For the Christian, the Church is definitely not just an exterior structure. The Church is the community of God, of His people, and where He gives Himself fully. To quote H. De Lubac: "Grace does not set up a purely individual relationship between the soul and God or Christ; rather, each one receives grace in the measure in which he is joined socially to that unique organism in which there flows its own life-giving stream. . . . All the sacraments are essentially 'sacraments in the Church'; in her alone they produce their full effect, for in her alone, 'the society of the Spirit,' is there, normally speaking, a sharing in the gift of the Spirit."[52] The task of this present section will be to find this bond of relationship between the Christian and the Church which is so intimate that, after he has sinned grievously, he must seek to be made one with her once again to enjoy the fruits of the Holy Spirit who dwells within her bosom. Why is it that the Christian, guilty of sin, must make reparation for the injury done to that body and be reconciled to her?[53]

The humanity of Christ is continued in the visible Church with its hierarchy, sacraments, cult, and dogma.[54] These visible

---

[50] S. Jaki, *Les Tendances Nouvelles de l'Ecclésiologie* (Paris, 1954), pp. 5–24; H. De Lubac, *Catholicism*, pp. 17–34; L. Cerfaux, *The Church in the Theology of St. Paul*, pp. 72–110.

[51] P. Palmer, "The Theology of the *Res et Sacramentum* with Particular Emphasis on its Application to Penance," in *Proceedings of the Catholic Theological Society of America*, 1959, p. 120.

[52] H. De Lubac, *Catholicism*, p. 35.

[53] Cf. R. Blomme, "Les Dimensions du Péché," in *Coll. Mech.*, 30 (1960), 571–579.   [54] Bossuet's definition of the Church: "Christ spread abroad and communicated."

elements help us to attain to the divine life. These sacraments are the Church's instruments. She is, moreover, the *Secundum Sacramentum* after the humanity of Christ Himself who is the *Primum Sacramentum*, the sign of God's love for men.[55] The Church, in continuing His work, is the continuous visible sign of God's love for men, the sacraments being a further visible extension of Christ in the Church. The sacraments belong essentially to the Church as her effective instruments. The Church, then, in turn has become the *Heilsgemeinschaft*, or the community of love and charity as it is expressed in Eph 4:15–16: "Rather by professing the truth, let us grow up in every respect in love and bring about union with Christ who is the head. The whole body is dependent on him. . . . In this way the body grows and builts itself up through love."[56] Therefore the Church is the place of charity, and the sacraments, her instruments, are means of beginning, increasing, or restoring this life and love.

It is evident, then, that being united to this community, participating in her love, the Christian not only sins against God but also against the Church, for charity is the life of the Church and he has reduced this means of charity in the Church. In the Church we are not alone; we find ourselves bound together in charity with the Blessed Trinity, together possessing a common divine life. My refusal given in sin is not just for God, but also for my brothers who are one with me in the same life and love. I have refused to live with them, associate with them in the one necessary condition of all: charity.[57]

Our sins not only vitiate our relations with others, but they actually attain others. How? Because we are essentially related to each other in the same Body. By baptism[58] we were brought together as members of this one Body.[59] This grace transforms

---

[55] Rom 5:6–11; 8:3; Jn 1:14, 18.

[56] See commentary on this text by L. Cerfaux in *The Church in the Theology of St. Paul*, p. 73.

[57] P. Ricoeur, "Morale sans Péché ou Péché sans Moralisme," in *Esprit* 22 (1954), 302.

[58] Canon 87, *Corporis Juris Canonici*.

[59] *Summa Theologiae*, II–II, q. 14., art. 2, ad 4.

us by a *gratia fraterna*, i.e., a grace which joins us into a community of persons (the Trinity and our neighbors in the Church).[60] By obligation as by privilege, we must live this grace in our daily lives, a grace which can fittingly be resumed in one word: love. Dynamically orientated toward others through fraternal grace we must carry this into daily life and living in sacrificing, giving, and helping the neighbor.[61] To sin is to destroy this whole essential relationship. It is to exist in a way that contradicts the way to which we are obliged by the essential fraternal grace which we possess. We have deprived the whole Body of our relation of love, our contribution, our "dynamism toward"; we have sinned against the whole body of the Church. "He has annihilated his capacity to communicate the influx of the Christian life."[62]

The interdependence of the different members of the Mystical Body of Christ is a favorite theme in St. Paul. "Just as in one body there are many members, all the members do not have the same function; so, too, we who are many are one body in Christ, the members of one another."[63] Paul continues, "No one lives for himself and no one dies for himself. If we live or if we die, we are the Lord's. For this Christ died and rose: that he be over both the living and the dead"; and later, "Rejoice with those who rejoice, weep with those who weep, together feeling the same thing."[64] In other words, Christ has give us the example. We must share all for the neighbor but in turn we depend on the neighbor for the graces needed for our task in the Church. Whether we be bishops or priests, mothers or

---

[60] A. Plé, "The Virtue of Charity," in *Love of Our Neighbor*, p. 78: ". . . Charity is 'totalitarian.' I cannot exclude a single one of its terms *cui* from my charity without thereby excluding all the rest. Either I love God, myself and all my brothers, known and unknown, or I love nobody. Certainly an act of love of God is distinct from an act of love on one's neighbors. But the act of the love of God includes love of the brethren at least implicitly. . . ."

[61] A. Plé, "The Bible on Brotherly Love," in *Love of Our Neighbor*, pp. 36–66.

[62] R. Blomme, *art. cit.*, p. 574.

[63] Rom 12:4. See also 1 Cor 12:27; Eph 4:25.

[64] Rom. 14:8–9; 12:15.

fathers, religious or laymen we depend essentially on each other. Individual sin deprives others of all this, possibly the grace of repentance for a sinner, the grace of resignation for a mother and father, etc. God alone knows what damage is brought to the Church by this sin. The Communion of Saints, of both persons and things, has been somewhat lessened by any refusal to love, to live dynamic relations, to offer for others in the one body which is the Church. In a sense, the flow of grace into the Body of the Church is lessened. The sinner is not only a dead cell in the Body for himself, but his disease spreads at least negatively by making no contribution to the vigor of the whole Body. He is not transmitting what God wants him to transmit. He is paralyzing God's work in many ways. He is guilty of a grave offense against the whole Body of the Church. Moreover, his bad disposition will, sooner or later, make itself known exteriorly. Sin is not only an internal thing. Having embodied itself in the soul, it naturally seeks (with the help of Satan) to incarnate itself in bad actions or dispositions, in concrete consequences. This bad disposition is bound to affect others for the worse. For just as "the good is diffusive of itself," so too is evil. This is a psychological fact that has always been noted by saintly men and women in the Church. It is in the nature of the human person to give external expression to that which is conceived within: the artist and his painting, the novelist and his novel, the businessman and his sales, the lovers and their love — all need and always acquire a certain form of external incarnation.[65] It becomes a ferment in exterior reality and enters the world of men. And it does not simply stop there: to use a simile of St. Thomas, as a stone thrown into the water causes ripples that will continue long after the stone is settled, so individual sin continues in the world by the bad influence it has on the many men who are to follow.

---

[65] St. Thomas: "Actio autem procedit ab agente, in rem exteriorem quam *transmutat,*" *De Veritate,* q. 7, art. 6, *in corpore;* H. Arendt, *The Human Condition,* pp. 155–223; P. Ricoeur, *La Philosophie de la Volunte,* Vol. I, p. 68; Nedoncelle, *Vers une Philosophie de l'Amour et de la Personne* (Paris, 1957), pp. 157–216.

"Sin does not attain just those who commit it; no sin, no matter how personal or secret it may be is limited to the sinner; we are united to all men as the members of a body and all has an effect on them which comes from us, good or evil. The 'good servant,' to repeat the gospel text, puts a new holy blood into the whole body; the man of sin weakens and infects and that is why when we confess our faults, we ask pardon not only of God, but of all our brother-men, as the bad workers who have spoiled the fruit of many labors . . . as the responsibles of a part of the evil which weakens many lives."[66] That is why the "and to you, brothers," which is recited daily before God's altar is not something fictitious; it is something real. The sinner has offended and weakened his brothers; the sinner has sinned against them. And just as in the days of old, we beg our brothers, in the second part of the *Confiteor*, to ask God to forgive us. In the Mystical Body of Christ, then, the effects of sin are social in nature. Its forgiveness, then, must, in a very real way, be social.

---

[66] P. Blanchet, "Doctrine Chrétienne du Péché," in *Monde Moderne et Sens du Péché*, p. 45.

PART II

God's Response: The Existence and Nature of Penance

CHAPTER V

The Notion of Penance in Scripture

INTRODUCTION

In order of importance after the notion of sin in Scripture is its complementary study, the notion of penance.[1] The two notions form one diptych in Scripture and one necessarily implies the other. The Fathers will later argue against the heretics "that penance will be done in vain if it lacks pardon."[2] If God threatens and entreats the sinner to do penance and to come back to the correct path, it is because God will pardon the sinner. Yet the sinner must reject his former decision for sin; he must condemn it and know, as did David, that "Against you only have I sinned." This return is called penance; it is painful and costly but its fruit is friendship with God in everlasting bliss.[3] The present chapter will describe this call to penance. It will not be out of place in this biblical study to add a small section on the history of penance in other types of religions outside the biblical context. In this way the preparation for penance will be seen in the very nature of man himself, the foundation on which God will place His supernatural call in Christ, His own Son.

I. CONFESSION AND REMISSION OF SINS BEFORE CHRIST

In a penetrating passage in the *Summa*, St. Thomas states, "It is of the natural law that man does penance for the evil he

---

[1] P. Anciaux, *Le Sacrément de la Pénitence* (Louvain, 1960), pp. 14–20; P. Galtier, *Aux Origines du Sacrément de Pénitence* (Rome, 1951), pp. 33–119; B. Poschmann, *Die Busse* (Bonn, 1940), pp. 14–120; also K. Rahner, *Die Kirche der Sünder*, pp. 24–106; *id.*, "Vergessene Wahrheiten über das Bussakrament," in *Geist und Leben*, 43 (1953), 340–343.

[2] Tertullian's *On Penance* (ed. Rauschen, *Florilegium Patristicum*, 10, 9).

[3] A. Descamps, "Le Péché dans le Nouveau Testament," in *Théologie du Péché* (Tournai, 1960), pp. 97–98.

has done . . . that he seeks to remedy the pain he has inflicted and that he show some sign of sorrow."[4] The Creator, for St. Thomas, has inscribed in man's very nature a need for some kind of forgiveness for the evil he has committed. In a sense, we may speak of a basis for the sacrament of penance in the very nature of man.

That this wise observation of St. Thomas is true is borne out by almost every ancient religious text which we still possess. Space and time do not permit an examination of them all. Besides, many of the texts have been already assembled in the work of Galtier.[5] The ancient Semitic tribes outside of Israel were studied by Pritchard, and his work clearly exhibits this penitential tendency.[6] Japan, China, India, and their representative religions, Confucianism, Brahmanism, Buddhism, Hinduism, each have an abundant literature on the confession and expiation of faults. "The promise of absolute pardon of sin is a sort of cliché common to all oriental and mystery religions. . . ."[7]

Father Galtier has analyzed the penitential literature in each of these religions and has come to the conclusion that "from the religious history of peoples before or foreign to Christianity it can be said that penance is of natural origin . . . that it is the first sign of the moral sense."[8] There are common examples of this in the confession of the Vedas, the therapeutic confession of the Buddhists, and the many psalms of penance among both Semites and Egyptians. Sacrifices and oblations sometimes accompany this penance, and it is commonly accepted that some form of punishment must accompany the act of confession. But the essential is the confession by which one appeases the gods.

In general, however, these pagan religions suffer from a com-

---

[4] III, q. 84, a. 7, ad 1.
[5] Aux Origines du Sacrément de Pénitence, pp. 1–32.
[6] Ancient Near East Texts Relating to the Bible (New Jersey, 1955), pp. 68–94.
[7] E. Brehier, Les Ideés Religieuses et Philosophiques de Philon, p. 307. See also J. Huby, ed., Christus: Manuel d'Histoire des Religions (Paris, 1947), pp. 361–371, 439–445, 688–692, etc.
[8] P. Galtier, op. cit., pp. 2–3.

mon malady. This is the tendency among these religions to make the practices of penance purely external in nature, corresponding little with the interior sentiments of the sinner. This danger of externalism, formalism, and juridicism was one that even the Jews of old were not able to escape, and we see the prophets attacking this notion of penance among the Chosen People. This externalism, in fact, is insoluble until we realize that the notion of a personal God before whom man is responsible for each of his actions is the basis of the prophetic teaching. Only Judaism and its fulfillment, Christianity, will be able to fill the gulf between the deity and man's personal and complete life. Pagan religions have a totally inadequate sense of penance because they are excessively concerned with a fear of offense connected to various external rites and practices rather than with love and fidelity to a personal God.

More to the point, however, is the sense of sin and its expiation in the Old Testament. The Hebrew vocabulary on sin is extraordinarily rich.[9] The concrete meaning of the words employed is indicative of the fact that God is considered as a living Person, with personal relationships between Himself and His people. This personal bond separates the Jews from their pagan neighbors who sought to appease their gods, usually personifications of nature, by a purely exterior cult and ritual. For the Jews, sin denotes an act hostile to God Himself which God cannot tolerate.[10] Sin is not simply an exterior act such as disregarding some external norm of morality set up by the gods. For the Jews it was certainly this, but much more: to sin was to fail God and ourselves. In the covenant, God established a personal relationship between Himself and Israel (a thing unheard of in any of the other ancient penitential texts) and to sin against this was to render oneself unfaithful to God's commandments.

Sin is a revolt against the manifest intentions of God, a direct

---

[9] Cf. C. Quell, *Theologische Wörterbuch*, I, pp. 268–269. Cf. *supra*, p. 9.

[10] J. Guillet, *Themes of the Bible* (Notre Dame, Ind., 1960), p. 97; A. George, "Le Sens du Péché dans l'Ancien Testament," in *Lumière et Vie*, 5 (1952), 22–25.

blow struck against a God who, by His covenant, has involved Himself in the world and has made Himself vulnerable.

> Woe to them, they have strayed from me!
>   Ruin to them, they have sinned against me!
> Though I wished to redeem them,
>   They spoke lies against me (Os 7:13).[11]

This interior guilt and renovation is present in the psalms. Accused by the prophet Nathan of his sin of adultery, David first confesses his personal sin to a personal God:

> Against you only have I sinned (Ps 50:6).[12]

But David is not left without hope of forgiveness, for in the same psalm we read:

> in the greatness of your Compassion wipe out my offense.
> Thoroughly wash me from my guilt and of my sin cleanse me (vv. 3–4).

This psalm clearly teaches that the interior aspect of repentance is the essential and that everything else is only a manifestation of this. Later verses of the same psalm substantiate this view of penance:

> v. 8: Behold, you are pleased with sincerity of heart,
>   and in my inmost being you teach me wisdom.
> v. 12: A clean heart create for me, O God,
>   and a steadfast spirit renew within me.
> v. 21: Then shall you be pleased with due sacrifices,
>   burnt offerings and holocausts;

The really important thing here is the notion of sin as a personal offense, a rejection of a person, of His love and fidelity. This is in direct contrast to the ritualistic and superstitious (in the full theological sense of this word) practice of pagan divinities.

The Jews, like the pagans, tried again and again to please God with a purely external rite — sacrifices and ritual were

---

11 Cf. also Ex 3:15; 6:9; 5:21; Os 8:1; 14:10; Mich 1:5; 3:8; 7:18, etc.
12 E. Kalt, *Herder's Commentary on the Psalms* (Westminster, Md., 1961), pp. 190–196.

offered in atonement for their offenses, and each time God rejected them:

> Listen to the instruction of our God, people of Gomorra!
> What care I for the number of your sacrifices?
>   says the Lord.
> I have had enough of whole-brunt rams and fat of fatlings;
> In the blood of calves, lambs and goats
>   I find no pleasure (Is 1:10–11).

Their repentance has to be real, internal, and loving. Nothing else would be acceptable to God. This, in general, is the theology of penance in the Old Testament.

But how did forgiveness take place in the Old Testament? Jewish forgiveness or knowledge of it was, in this respect, on the same level as that of the pagans; they had no absolute assurance that their sins were forgiven.[13] Their sense of culpability and their strongly felt need for forgiveness were the same as that of other men.[14] Most theologians agree with St. Thomas[15] that there were no real sacraments (ex opere operato) in the Old Testament, but that these rites were simply protestations of faith in the coming Savior. As expressions of faith, God accepted them (ex opere operantis) with their interior aspirations of repentance and external sacrifice.[16] The law received its efficacy from these sensible signs (confession, ritual, sacrifice, etc.) through which the Jews gave their implicit faith in Christ whose salvific power they anticipated. In the words of Galtier,[17] "The material elements (of the Christian sacraments) already existed. Washings and ablutions, anointing with oil and imposition of hands were of daily use in Israel. . . . For them to become properly sacramental, it was sufficient for them to receive from Christ the supernatural virtue which the Catholic Church recognizes

---

[13] H. Gavin, *The Jewish Antecedents of the Christian Sacraments* (London, 1951), pp. 18–21.

[14] J. Bonsivren, *Le Judaisme Palestinien*, II (Paris, 1948), pp. 92–105.

[15] III, q. 84, a. 7, ad 2.

[16] Rom 3:19; 7:1; 7:7; 8:2; Gal 2:16; 3:5; 10; 4:4, etc. See M. J. Lagrange, *Epître aux Romains* (Paris, 1950), p. 70 ff.

[17] Galtier, *op. cit.*, p. 38.

in them. . . . They (the sacraments of the Old Law) were signs
and they helped to obtain the religious reality they symbolized."

II. The Notion of Penance in the New Testament in General

A detailed analysis of the New Testament is not necessary to
this study; it is only necessary to demonstrate that the notion of
penance existed and that Christ gave special power and control
of penance to the Apostles.[18]

From the first moment of His public life, Christ teaches that
the Kingdom has come and therefore penance must be performed
(Mk 1:5). With Christ, the last times have begun and the
eschatological Kingdom is present. Penance, the metanoia, must
turn man's whole orientation toward the Kingdom present with
Christ (Mk 2:10). To be saved, it is sufficient to believe in
Jesus and He will pardon the really great evil in our lives, sin
(Lk 7:36). Christ not only performs external miracles over the
sick, but restores health to the soul killed by sin (Lk 5:31).
And Christ tells us explicitly: "Unless you do penance, you will
all likewise perish" (Lk 13:1). This appeal to conversion must
be heard and adhered to if we want to come to Christ (Lk
10:16). We must listen to His words, that His Kingdom is not
of this earth, and that He leads to divine and eternal life by way
of suffering and death.

The Jews misunderstood this message of salvation and were
rejected (Lk 24:45). Recognizing Jesus, man had to recognize
himself as sinner, and that he could not serve two masters,
Christ and the world (Mt 6:24). Christ gives the opening into
the Kingdom which will deliver man from the slavery of Satan
(Mt 21:29-32). This conversion of life must change our lives.
It implies a complete turning from ourselves to God (Mt 28:3).

---

[18] For a more detailed study of the New Testament see W. Lange,
"L'Appel à la Pénitence dans le Christianisme Primitif," in *Coll. Mech.*,
29 (1959), 380–390; Poschmann, *Poenitentia Secunda*, pp. 50–75; Galtier,
op. cit., pp. 35–106.

The message of salvation, then, includes the essential message of conversion. But Christ founded an apostolic community which received its mission from Him to continue His own work, giving it power to chase out devils, to heal the sick, and to forgive the brother who repents (Mt 18:3; Mk 9:33).

After His resurrection, Christ promised the Apostles that He would send the Holy Spirit who would animate the whole of the Church (Acts 2:4). Entrance into this community would be conditioned by penance and by faith in the risen Christ, for men are sinners. This apostolic mission begins on Pentecost and the events prophesied by the prophets for the last times were to bear witness to that event (Acts 2:7; 3:10). Some listened and believed; they did penance and were baptized. Others mocked. The visible effects or signs, miracles, etc., prove that the last times have arrived and salvation is offered to those who believe and do penance (Acts 3:12; 4:8; 5:29; 10:34). The kerygma or message of salvation is announced everywhere by the Apostles: Jesus is the envoy of God, the Messias. The Jews killed Him, but God has raised Him up to fulfill Scripture and the prophets, and sits now at the right hand of the Father (Acts 5:31). The Apostles make their appeal to penance, then, by exhortations, by threats, and by direct appeal (Acts 2:40; 10:42; 18:5; 20:21). Salvation in the name of Jesus is not reserved for the Jews, but for all men (Acts 3:26). This is manifest to St. Peter in the conversion of Cornelius (Acts 9:31). Jewish practices are no longer imposed on the Gentile converts (Acts 9:5; 1:38; 15:11). This will leave Paul a completely free hand in his preaching to the pagans. God now has mercy on Jew and Gentile alike. The time has come for the pagans, too, to repent of their past blindness and be converted and live in Christ. The calling of the pagans to penance forms an essential part of the apostolic preaching. This becomes yet a further testimony of God's love, realized in its fullness in the resurrection of Christ for all men. Conversion is thus a gift of God: Jesus aiding the sinner to repent (Acts 3:26; 7:21). But penance is also man's work (Acts 2:40).

Conversion must take place. The sinner must orient himself to God in an engagement of total faith. It is not a conversion to *something* but to *someone* by the power of the Spirit (Acts 8:21). Men must repent and be converted, since these two actions go essentially together — repentance and pardon, repentance and faith, repentance and new life (Acts 2:38; 20:21; 11:18). These two aspects of penance, repentance and conversion, are preached with vigor in the primitive Christian kerygma. To be attached to Christ, a spiritual poverty, humility, self-detachment is necessary. Conversion implies obedience and fidelity to Christ who saves and liberates man from sin (Acts 4:12; 5:29). For the pagans, penance is a return to the true God, and this implies an abandonment of the life of sin (Acts 14:15; 15:19; 26:18). This will insure the convert of life eternal and entrance into the Messianic Kingdom (Acts 11:18; 3:19).

But this conversion and refusal to sin is not an isolated and decisive act. It is a continuous struggle which demands a continuous vigilance (Acts 20:31). There is constant danger of returning to previous faults. This *metanoia* or conversion implies a changing of a person's whole orientation of life and sentiments. It is a transmutation of the spirit and of the heart, a complete interior renovation, full of confidence in the merciful God. This requires, above all, an individual's free decision, a sincere engagement and an option for God which leaves no doubt. The recourse is ours.

Some will welcome it, embrace it with a full heart in faith by baptism in Christ's name in the community of the saved under the guidance of the Church of God (Acts 20:28). Others will continue in their obstinate infidelity and be confirmed in their sins (Acts 8:23). They will persecute the Church and her leaders and inflict all manner of injury against Christ and His disciples (Acts 5:21; 13:50).

All these notions will receive greater development in the Epistles of St. Paul as well as those of St. John. But this is the essential message of penance and conversion in the early Christian kerygma. It remains true to itself throughout the whole tradition of the Church from the earliest days until the present. The *metanoia* was as necessary for the first Christians as it was for those of today. The call to penance has always and will always remain essentially the same; only its modes can change.

III. THE DIRECT PROMISES OF CHRIST IN REGARD TO PENANCE

Our present problem is more particularly the specific texts of the New Testament in which Christ gave the power to forgive and retain sin. Following are the texts to which the Fathers will have recourse in defending the right of the Church to forgive any and every sin. They are:

> *1 Cor 5:1 ff:* "There is a widespread report of immorality in your midst and . . . what is worse, you are arrogant! . . . As for me, though absent in body, I am present in spirit, and have already, as if present, reached the decision. . . . You and my spirit, gathered in the name of our Lord Jesus Christ . . . decree by the authority of our Lord Jesus Christ, to deliver this man to Satan for the destruction of his corrupt tendencies that his spirit may attain salvation on the day of the Lord Jesus."
>
> *Mt 18:15–18:* The admonition given to a brother who has sinned and his final "excommunication" by the Church and in which Christ concludes: "I tell you with assurance: whatever you bind on earth shall be bound in heaven; whatever you loose on earth shall be loosed in heaven."
>
> *Mt 16:17–20:* "You are Peter . . . I will give you the keys of the kingdom of heaven, and whatever you bind on earth shall be bound in heaven, and whatever you loose on earth shall be loosed in heaven."
>
> *Jn 20:22–23:* "With this, he breathed on them and said: 'Receive the Holy Spirit. Whenever you remit anyone's sins, they are remitted; when you retain anyone's sins, they are retained.' "[19]

In the text of St. John, the argument is based on the fact that Christ is addressing the Apostles alone, a fact evident from the

---

[19] This text was defined as such by the Council of Trent, D.B. 913. The text, the Council stated, was always understood in the Church as referring to the forgiveness of sins in the Sacrament of Penance. Schröder, *op. cit.*, p. 89.

context.[20] Both clauses are in strict relation with each other as is evident in the Greek rhythm: the protasis and apodasis in each clause. Christ can only mean a true forgiveness of sin and an extension of His own action which He performed while on earth. It is quite true, as the old reformers maintained,[21] that if only the protasis were present, the text could be well understood in a general way as the forgiving of sins by the spreading of the good word (Lk 24:44–48). It is evident, however, from the context that these words of St. John are not to be understood in a general way, but in a very specific way; the Apostles' action would have the same effect in heaven as it has on earth, and it is dependent on their judgment alone: if they reconcile a sinner, this also happens in heaven; if they refuse to reconcile a sinner, this also happens in heaven. Both elements of the proposition have the same object: the forgiveness or retention of sin (*aphêontai*). The use of the perfect tense in Greek signifies an accomplished fact. Thus sinners are given the assurance of divine forgiveness in the measure that this power is exercised by the Apostles.[22]

The most interesting texts from an exegetical and sacramental point of view are those addressed to the Apostles (Mt 18:15) and to St. Peter alone (Mt 16:17). Quite reasonably, these two texts will be used time and time again throughout Christian tradition in direct reference to the Apostles' power to forgive sin. The only two noteworthy exceptions will be Tertullian, the Montanist,[23] and Peter Abelard, who later retracted his original meaning.[24] The fact remains, however, that this was the unanimous interpretation of these texts for almost fifteen hundred years.

---

[20] For a detailed study of each of these texts in relation to the forgiveness of sins see B. Xiberta, *Clavis Ecclesiae*, pp. 13–22; Galtier, *op. cit.*, pp. 43–91; *De Poenitentia* (Roma, 1940), pp. 98–109.

[21] H. Zahn, *Das Evangelium des Johannes*, pp. 680–681. Also J. Munck, *Petrus und Paulus in der Offenbarung Johannes*, p. 627 ff.

[22] B. Xiberta, *Clavis Ecclesiae* (Rome, 1924), p. 16.

[23] *On Modesty* (ed. Rauschen, FIP, 10, 21).

[24] *Ethics* (P.L., 178, c. 672); see also C. Ottaviano, "Frammenti Abelardiani," in *Rivista di Cultura*, 12 (1931), 442.

We have already seen the primitive context in which Christ spoke these momentous words to St. Peter and the rest of the Apostles.[25] It was in the context of the ecclesial parables about the Kingdom. The Apostles are commissioned, and in a special sense delegated, to continue the work of the Kingdom on earth. They are Christ's legates and representatives, and as a token of this very fact, they receive the power to forgive or to retain sin. It will be recalled that Christ establishes the Kingdom by His very presence; He is the Son of Man (Dn 7:6) who comes from heaven with godly powers: since He is from heaven and since the Kingdom has begun with Him, a sure sign of the Kingdom's presence is that "devils are cast out," which is another way of saying that sins are forgiven. The Apostles are Christ's delegates, they are instructed to continue the Kingdom, and therefore Christ gives them the power to forgive sins. The Kingdom is the Church, and within the Church Christ's representatives forgive sin in Christ's place. Thus the principle of modern exegetes is fully justified: any affirmation can be understood only in function of a concrete problem to be resolved; it can never be isolated to act as the major or minor premise of a theological theorem outside the space and time of the concrete situation.[26] Thus authors are fully justified in giving the Apostles power in the Church over sins in virtue of these two texts, a real power to "bind and to loose."[27]

The second analysis of the text, however, must proceed from an intrinsic meaning of the words and phrases themselves. It is here that history and philology serve both the exegete and the theologian. According to the famous Protestant New Testament scholar, F. Buschel,[28] the word or metaphor "bind and loose" can have three distinct meanings: (1) the magical power of casting

[25] *Supra*, pp. 31–32.

[26] A. Descamps, art. cit., *Théologie* . . . , pp. 49–50.

[27] A. Descamps, "La Methode en Théologie Biblique," in *Sacra Pagina*, I, pp. 138–148.

[28] *Wörterbuch zum Neuen Testament*, II, 59 ff. For full treatment see F. Abrist, *Echtheitsfrage und Deutung der Primatsstelle, Mt 16, 18 f in der Deutschen Protestantischen Theologie* (Munster-en-w., 1961).

a spell over a person and then releasing him; (2) the legislative power granted a rabbi or teacher of declaring what was forbidden (bound) or permitted (loosed) in the Mosaic law; (3) the juridical power of judging an individual and of imposing a ban or excommunication (to bind) and of afterward restoring or reconciling the excommunicate to the community (to loose). Only the third meaning of "bind and loose" is appropriate for understanding (Mt 18:15). It is, moreover, a meaning upon which all Catholic and non-Catholic authors agree.[29] The power given the Apostles is therefore a legislative and a juridical power; in other words, whom the Church excludes God excludes, whom the Church reconciles to herself God reconciles to Himself.

In the saying of Jesus reported by St. Matthew in 16:13, St. Peter (Aramaic; *foundation, rock*) is placed as the head of the Church in a very particular way.[30] In virtue of this special power, he is given absolute power to forgive sin in the Kingdom. "The gates of Hell" is a personification of the powers of evil which attempt to trap men in eternal death. The mission of the Church will then be to deliver men from this valley of death — which is sin — and to do this, it is given the power to forgive sin in the person of St. Peter. In Christ's name, then, Peter will open and close these gates of salvation. Peter, as the chief custodian of the Church, is given the keys (which represent power) of God's house. His decisions will be ratified by God in heaven and a relationship of equality is set up in both phrases, bind and loose.

Most non-Catholic exegetes either omit the text as a later interpolation[31] or hold that this power was a personal gift given only to the Apostles and St. Peter.[32] Admittedly, the text itself

---

[29] P. Palmer, *Sources of Christian Theology*, II (Westminster, Md., 1959), p. 3.

[30] P. Benoit, "La Primauté de Pierre," in *Revue Biblique*, 58 (1956), 258–264.

[31] Among others, see Th. Zahn, *Das Evangelium des Matthaeus*, ad hoc; J. Hering, *Le Royaume de Dieu et sa Venue*, p. III ff.; R. Bultmann, *Theology of the New Testament*, I, p. 45; E. Stauffer, "Zur Vor und Frühgeschichtes des Primatus Petri," in *ZKG*, 36 (1943–1944), p. 1 ff.

[32] O. Cullmann, *Peter Disciple, Apostle, Martyr* (London, 1953), pp. 155–212.

does not indicate whether it is to be given to the Apostles' successors or not, but most Catholic theologians and exegetes argue that it is legitimate to suppose that this certainly was the intention of Jesus in establishing the principles and basis for the Kingdom. Exegetically, the fact that the Kingdom is set up by Christ implies that Christ wishes the Church to continue Ilis mission. Now one of the essential traits of the Kingdom is the forgiveness of sin, and for that very reason, the power to forgive sin in the successors of the Apostles is certainly an implicit connotation of the establishment of the Kingdom.[33] This seems to be the teaching of Scripture and has been interpreted in this way by Christian tradition through the ages.

CONCLUSION

Exegetically, these texts, especially those of Jn 20:22 and Mt 16:18, can certainly mean that the Apostles have the actual power in the Church, to the exclusion of all others, to forgive sin or not to forgive sin. Their judgment will be accepted before God, and no one shall receive forgiveness from God unless it comes first through the Apostles.[34] Their judgment must precede. All these texts, are, moreover, attested to by the oldest manuscripts and can hardly be interpolations. But even if these texts were not so clear, the Church as a whole always understood them as such. Even the heretics of the third and fourth centuries, such as the Montanists and the Novatians, never denied that these texts referred to the power of the Church's leaders to forgive and retain sins. Whom the Church excludes, God excludes; whom the Church reconciles to herself, God reconciles to Himself. This is the interpretation of the Gospel texts by all of tradition for the first fifteen hundred years of the Church's existence.

---

[33] For further information see P. Benoit, *L'Evangile Selon St. Matthieu* (La Sainte Bible de Jerusalem), pp. 104–105.

[34] These texts should definitely exclude those Protestants who were of the opinion that only the "sancti" and not sinners were part of the primitive Church. Cf. A. Harnack, *Die Mission und Ausbreitung*, t. II, pp. 209–225; F. Loofs, *Leit Faden zur Dogmengeschichte*, p. 205. See also the magnificent work of H. Schlier, *Le Temps de l'Eglise* (Tournai, 1961).

CHAPTER VI

A Short History of the Sacrament of Penance

INTRODUCTION

The history of the sacrament of penance is one of the most complicated as well as the most illuminating of studies. It is complicated because the form in which the sacrament was administered for nearly 500 years was quite different from the form with which we are now acquainted. The evolution of the structures of this sacrament, at first glance, creates the impression that not only has the form changed but that the very sacrament itself is different today than it was in the first five centuries of the Church. This was at least the charge made by the non-Catholic liberal historians and scholars at the turn of this century.[1] Yet, a more detailed study of the historical sources of this sacrament proves just the opposite of that which our Protestant brothers would have us believe. It will show beyond any shadow of doubt that the fundamental structure of the sacrament of penance remains essentially the same today as it was in the early centuries of the Church.[2] The work of such eminent Catholic

---

[1] See the various works by Protestant scholars. A. Harnack, *Lehrbuch der Dogmengeschichte*, I, pp. 439–444. See also his *Outlines of the History of Dogma* (Boston, 1957), pp. 399–405; O. D. Watkins, *A History of Penance*, I, pp. 103–126; R. C. Mortimer, *The Origins of Private Penance*, I (London, 1920), pp. 53–64.

[2] For our source material for this chapter, we have used the translations of Paul F. Palmer, *Sources of Christian Theology*, II (Westminster, 1959).

scholars as Morin,[3] Petau,[4] Poschmann,[5] Galtier,[6] Adam and D'Ales[7] has proven this point beyond any reasonable doubt. The sacrament has undergone, then, a considerable evolution in its administration. It is only in the twelfth century (the early scholastic period) that we have a systematic and theological formulation of penance as a sacrament along with an analysis and description of its constitutive elements.[8] This is the form and elaboration with which we are acquainted today and which has remained rather stable in the West. Hence, our study must concentrate on the first eleven centuries, noting the evolution and basic elements of this sacrament.[9] This will be the objective of this section.

I. Earliest Testimonies

The earliest references to penance are very few in number before the third century.[10] The reason for this was probably the fervor of the first Christians who were constantly being persecuted throughout these years. To read the Epistles of St. Paul, one would think this to be true in spite of the fact that all was

---

[3] See his now famous study in positive theology of the sacrament of penance, *Commentarius Historicus de Disciplinà in Administratione Sacramenti Poenitentiae, Tredecim Primis Saeculis in Ecclesia Occidentali et Hucusque in Orientali Observata* (Paris, 1651).

[4] *De Poenitentia Publica et Preparatione ad Communionem,* in his *Dogmata Theologica* (Paris, 1867).

[5] A number of these works exist only in German; no English translations as yet. *Die Abendlandische Kirchenbusse in Früher Mittelalter* (Breslau, 1930); *Die Busse* (Freiburg-im-Br., 1951); *Poenitentia Secunda* (Bonn, 1950); etc.

[6] *Aux Origines du Sacrément de Pénitence* (Romae, 1951); *De Poenitentia Tractatus Dogmatico Historicus* (Romae, 1950); *L'Eglise et la Remission des Péchés aux Premiers Siècles* (Paris, 1952).

[7] His famous *L'Edit de Calliste* (Paris, 1913) was one of the main elements in the Catholic revival of historical studies on penance in the early Church.

[8] P. Anciaux, *La Théologie du Sacrément de Pénitence au XII Siècle* (Louvain, 1949), pp. 56–104; this work is probably the most complete study of the theological formulation of the sacrament of penance in the early scholastic period.

[9] P. Anciaux, *Le Sacrément de la Pénitence* (Louvain, 1960), pp. 53–64.

[10] P. Galtier, "La Pratique Penitentielle à l'Âge Apostolique," in his *Aux Origines du Sacrément de Pénitence*, pp. 62–106.

not perfect in these early Christian communities.[11] It can be said, however, that during this initial period, the times are those of Christian fervor where the discipline of penance was not in full vigor as a deterrent to sin. This latter element will become more pronounced in later centuries.[12] The community was steeped in fraternal charity and therefore the spirit of forgiveness and clemency was more in vogue. This was the theme of the famous Catholic historian of penance, Jean Morin: ". . . if we turn our attention to the very beginnings of the Church's history, we shall find that the attitude of the Church towards sinners is progressively more clement and lenient."[13]

Another strong reason for the suprising silence of these first years with regard to penance is the fact that it was simply accepted as part of the Christian life. It was a time of "peaceful possession," when no one doubted either its existence or its efficacy in the Church.[14] The documents on penance increase greatly only when it was attacked by the Montanist and Novatian heretics of the third and fourth centuries. It was only natural, then, in view of these errors that the Fathers would come to the doctrinal defense of penance as an institution of Christ in the Church.

In any case, one of the earliest documents on penance is that of The Shepherd of Hermas about the year 140.[15] The value of this document lies in the witness it gives of the Roman practice of penance in the early second century. The document should prove to all that the Church was not just simply the "Church of saints" from which sinners were excluded. On the contrary,

---

[11] See 1 Cor 5:1–5 where St. Paul actually excommunicated a public sinner; many authors claim that this is the same person whom Paul reconciles in 2 Cor 2:6–8; for consensus of opinion see the monumental work on the subject by E. B. Allo, *Première Epître aux Corinthiens* (Paris, 1956), pp. 121–127.

[12] Father Galtier would seem to hold the opposite view, *op. cit.*, pp. 12–16; Morin is of the same opinion as the present author. Cf. Morin, *op. cit.*, IV, IX, 1.

[13] Morin, *ibid.*

[14] J. Lebreton and J. Zeiller, *Histoire de l'Église, de la Fin du 2 Siècle à la Paix Constantinienne*, II (Paris, 1948), pp. 353–360.

[15] *The Shepherd of Hermas*, ed. Funk, I, 362, 394, 396.

the subject of part of this document is to offer hope of pardon even to those Christians who, although regenerated once in baptism, have fallen into some grievous sin.[16]

> I have heard, sir, said I, from certain teachers that there is no other repentance than the one when we went down into the water and received remission of our former sins. He said to me, you have heard correctly for so it is. He who has received remission of sin ought never to sin again, but to live in purity. But since you ask diligently about all things, I will explain this also to you, not as giving excuse to those who in the future shall believe or to those who already believe in the Lord. For those who have already believed or are about to believe have no repentance of sins, but have remission of their former sins . . . the Lord therefore being full of mercy and compassion on this creation has established this repentance and to me was given the power over this repentance. But I tell you, said he, after that great and solemn calling, if a man should be tempted by the devil and sin, he has one repentance. But, if he sin repeatedly and repent, it is unprofitable for such a man for hardly shall he live. . . .[17]

From this passage, it is evident that there is a power in the Church to forgive serious sin committed after baptism. This forgiveness is not restricted to so-called "irremissible sins," but the document expressly mentions two sins which later heretics will claim are not within the power of the Church to forgive: adultery and apostasy. "Those, then who are willing to do penance, will be strong in faith." And to the husband of the woman who has committed adultery, the Angel of the Shepherd admonishes him "to take her back, after penance has been performed."

The reconciliation of the sinner is in the power of the Church. In other words, to be pleasing to God, sinners must be once again incorporated into the Church from which they have been somehow cast out by their sins: "If they fail to be integrated into the Tower (the Church) they will be permanently rejected. For this reason (sin) they have been rejected and cast aside from the tower. Those, then who are willing to do penance if

---

[16] J. Quasten, *Patrology*, I (Westminster, Md., 1950), pp. 98–99.
[17] *The Shepherd* . . . , I, 394.

they actually perform it will be strong in the Faith if they do
penance now while the tower is being built. But if the tower
is finished, there is no longer a place for them, instead they will
be outcasts."[18] The doctrine of penance in Hermas is already
thoroughly permeated with the idea that the Church is an instrument necessary for salvation. The author of this treatise goes on
to speak of the prayer offered for sinners by the elders of the
Church, and it is very likely that reconciliation with and through
the Church is at least implicit in this prayer.[19] This, however,
is uncertain.

The most serious problem which confronts Catholic historians
of penance of this period is the unicity of penance (i.e., could be
performed but once) in the early Church. This problem is not
restricted to Hermas but becomes a part and parcel of the whole
penitential discipline of the early Church. Could serious sins
(adultery, idolatry, and murder) be repented for just once? If
a Christian who had done penance for one of these crimes committed the same crime, was he forever excluded from reconciliation with the Church and therefore with God? This is probably
the most perplexing problem for any historian of penance. Catholic authors are divided on this point, but there seems to be
strong evidence that these three sins were accorded only one
forgiveness.[20] If these sins were committed again, sinners were
not forgiven but left to the mercy of God.[21] In any case, whether
the Church reconciled these sinners for a second time or not
was purely a matter of discipline, not doctrine. The Church was
always conscious of her power to forgive "seventy times seven."
The reason for this single opportunity of penance (as in our
present text) is more psychological than doctrinal. "The pastoral
difficulty of encouraging sin by stressing the possibility of pardon

---

[18] Ibid., 362.
[19] P. Palmer, Sources of Christian Theology, II, Sacraments and Forgiveness, p. 12; A. D'Ales, op. cit., p. 112.
[20] G. H. Joyce, "Private Penance in the Early Church," in Journal of
Theological Studies, 42 (1953), 22–26.
[21] See the texts of Popes Innocent I and Leo I which we shall cite
later in this chapter.

was sensed more acutely in the early Church and may explain much of the harsher legislation of the early discipline of penance."[22] Yet, we will notice a tendency to greater clemency for all types of sinners, even for those who had fallen more than once into these three gravest sins. We must admit, however, that "it is the absence of a private penitential discipline even for lesser sins that led to the complete decadence of morals in the late fifth and sixth centuries and to the almost complete abandonment of the sacrament as the ordinary remedy for sin to be made use of in time of health."[23] It would seem, however, that penance for these major sins could be performed but once.

A second important witness of the early Church is the story told by Clement of Alexandria. Whether it be true or not (Clement attests to its truthfulness) it shows at least the attitude of the Church toward sinners at the very beginning of the third century (215). The story is told that St. John, after his release from the Island of Patmos, visited the city of Ephesus where he had earlier entrusted a promising young man to the care of the bishop. It seems that the young man became involved with a band of robbers and was made their chief. On hearing what had happened, St. John sent out to find the young man, whereupon he was taken prisoner by the robbers and taken to their leader who, upon recognizing St. John, sought to flee. He was overtaken by the Apostle and led back to penance.

> When the old man approached, the robber embraced him, confessing the while as best he could with loud sobs and concealing his right hand (a figure for his sins) he was baptized anew in his tears. Then he (St. John), so they say, assured him on oath that he had found pardon for him from the Savior, and knelt and kissed his hand as now cleansed by his repentance, and led him back to the Church. And then making supplication with a wealth of prayers, he vied with him in protracted fasts, and soothing his troubled mind with many words, he did not leave him, so they say, until he had re-established him in the Church. . . .[24]

[22] Palmer, *op. cit.*, p. 14.

[23] P. Palmer, "Jean Morin and Private Penance," in *Theological Studies*, 5 (Sept., 1945), 356.

[24] *Who is the Rich Man That is Saved?* (*Die Griechischen Christlichen Schriftsteller der Ersten Drei Jahrhundert*, XVII, 190).

The Apostle vied in fasts until he "was re-established in the Church." This presupposes that this was in some way connected with the fact that John "had found pardon for him from the Savior."

It is interesting to note two things about the story: even as late as the third century this story forms abundant evidence that the Church reconciled a murderer to herself. This will serve as direct evidence against Tertullian and the Montanists who made the novel distinction between remissible and irremissible sins. In reality, then, it is the heretics who introduce a nontraditional distinction in this regard. The second point in question brought out by this story is that the sinner is reconciled to the Church, the understood sign of God's own pardon (at least that is presupposed by the author of the story). Yet it remains true that Clement is also a witness to the unicity of penance in the Church and its growing rigorism in the matter of penitential discipline. It would be too tedious to cite all of the texts in this regard.

The beginning of the third century witnesses the rise of the first heresies which deny various elements of the penitential discipline.[25] Montanism and Novatianism, two rigorist heresies, denied that the Church has received the power to forgive the "irremissible" sins (adultery, idolatry, and murder).

Montanism was essentially an ecclesiological heresy putting prophetism above the episcopal hierarchy. The heresy was founded in Phrygia about the year 170 by Montanus, who was favored with various mystical ecstasies. The disciples (notably women) were supposed to communicate directly with the Spirit in various states of ecstatic trances. The normal outcome was that the Spirit ruled the community directly by these illuminated prophets (pneumatics) and not through the normally constituted episcopal hierarchy in the Church (psychics, *numerum Episcoporum*). Thus prophetism is put above the hierarchy. A second element

---

[25] For a history of these heresies see F. Cayré, *Manual of Patrology and History of Theology*, I (Paris, 1935), pp. 250–254; J. Lebreton and J. Zeiller, *Histoire* . . . , pp. 35–41; also superficial work of H. Lietzmann, *A History of the Early Church*, I (New York, 1961), pp. 227–257.

in their doctrine was a belief in the imminent Parousia, or the second coming of Christ. It will be remembered that that belief characterized various communities which St. Paul himself had to correct (2 Thes 2:1–8; 3:6–13). In any case, this belief naturally led to rigorism in matters of penance and matrimony. Second marriages were branded as adultery and "unforgivable" sins were introduced into the penitential discipline.

The most famous convert to this heresy was the great lawyer and apologist, Tertullian. As a Catholic, he wrote a splendid treatise on penance called *De poenitentia*, in which the normal Catholic teaching is given.[26] It reflects a spirit of clemency which was in the tradition of the first two centuries. He makes no distinction between forgivable and unforgivable sins and exhorts all to penance no matter what their sins might have been. "He [Christ] reproves those of Pergamum for teaching perverse doctrines; He castigates those of Laodicea for putting trust in riches. And yet He exhorts all to penance, even under threat. Now He would not threaten the impenitent unless He were ready to forgive the penitent."[27] Tertullian goes on to explain that penance, however, must be done in the Church and it is the Church who forgives through the *exomologesis* or confession. It is uncertain whether it was made to the whole congregation or, as is more likely, to the bishop. In any case, the penitent must confess in the Church. "The body cannot rejoice over the misery of one of its members, rather the whole body must suffer and work together for the cure. The Church is present in one and the next, and the Church is truly Christ. . . . Is it better to be damned in secret than to be absolved in public?"[28] This confession is not simply an external formula empty of efficacy; rather it reaches to the depths of the soul, forgiving the eternal punishment which has been incurred by grievous sin: ". . . that by passing judgment on the sinner, it [exomologesis] may of itself act as a substitute

---

[26] See the introduction and commentary on these treatises by W. P. Le Saint, *Tertullian: Treatises on Penance* (Ancient Christian Writers, 1959).

[27] *On Penance*, trans. by W. P. Le Saint, *op. cit.*, p. 30.

[28] *Ibid.*, p. 31.

for God's warth, and by temporal punishment, I will not say frustrate, but rather discharge the eternal penalties."[29]

Tertullian, as a Montanist, will deny the truth of what he has written as a Catholic. In his heretical treatise *On Modesty* he says: "I am no longer ashamed of my error, which I have rejected, since I rejoice in having rejected it, and find myself the better and the purer for having done so. . . . No one is ashamed of having taken a step forward."[30] His wrath is directed against the so-called "edict of Callistus," probably of the bishop of Rome, who claimed to absolve even adulterers after penance had been performed. We shall not enter into Tertullian's invective, but the treatise serves a valuable purpose for the history of the early penitential discipline. Indirectly, it shows us the Catholic position through Tertullian's attacks.[31] The Catholic position is that all sins can find pardon since all sinners are encouraged to do penance. Thus the Catholic position, which Tertullian attacks, is based on the doctrine of the keys which were given to Peter and the Apostles and by them to their successors, the bishops of the Catholic Church.

Tertullian's distinction between forgivable and unforgivable sins confronts us with something entirely new, something without precedent in the primitive penitential discipline. Tertullian introduces an unheard-of distinction among sins; as we saw, it was a logical deduction from the Montanist rigorism in matters of penance. Yet, on the other hand, the heresy could not have been entirely new since it was argued and accepted by a great number of former Catholics turned Montanist or Novatian; the problem is solved if we consider that all during the primitive history of penance, the unicity of penance for these three major crimes (*crimina*) was a strict canonical rule. It is evident, then, that the Montanist and Novatian heretics had but one step to take: to claim that this rigorism was not a disciplinary function but one of doctrine. Thus, with this precedent in the primitive

29 *Ibid.*
30 *On Modesty*, trans. by W. P. Le Saint, *op. cit.*, p. 55.
31 Palmer, *op. cit.*, p. 27.

discipline, it is easy to see how logical the claim of the heretics sounded to many Catholics: the Church in reality had received no power to forgive these three major crimes. By an ironic turn of history, then, Tertullian foreshadows the Protestant error that God alone, not the bishops of the Catholic Church, can forgive sins. "For the right and the decision (to forgive sins) belongs to the Lord, and not to the servant, to God Himself, not to the priest."[32]

Tertullian thus serves as one of the surest witnesses of the penitential practice of the Catholic Church in the early third century; the Church can reconcile all sinners to itself after penance in virtue of the power given to the bishops of the Catholic Church to bind and loose.

Our final witness of this early period is St. Cyprian.[33] To state the case to the point of oversimplification, St. Cyprian progressed in his thought concerning the forgiveness of the three major sins.[34] In one of his earlier epistles, he says that "certain bishops thought that it was impossible to reconcile [dare pacem] an adulterer. But as long as they respect the unity of the Church, each Bishop is free as to how he himself acted, since he is responsible for his acts." In other words, Cyprian clearly distinguishes between *theory* and *practice*. In theory, the Church had the power to reconcile such sinners. In practice, it was up to the injured bishops, responsible before God, to act more or less severely according to the circumstances. The principal reason for rigorism was that it would act as a deterrent to others. In his other writings, Cyprian himself allowed a time for penance followed by reconciliation for adulterers. St. Cyprian, furthermore, distinguishes between the sins against men and the sins against God. These latter (apostasy, idolatry) were not recon-

[32] *On Modesty* (ed. Rauschen, Forilegium Patristicum, 10, 31–96).

[33] For text of the *Lapsed* see the introduction and translation by M. Bevenot (Ancient Christian Writers, N. 25). For other texts see Palmer, *op. cit.*, pp. 42–47; B. Poschmann, *Handbuch der Dogmengeschichte*, IV, 3, and in his *Poenitentia Secunda*, pp. 398–424.

[34] K. Rahner, "Die Busslehre des hl. Cyprian Von Kathago," in ZKT, 74 (1952), 257–276.

ciled. It is commonly agreed among scholars that prior to the
Decian persecution, Cyprian regarded these sins as irremissible.
But with the outbreak of that persecution, Cyprian ceased to act
according to his personal views, and, as we shall see, even the
apostates were later exhorted to penance and pardon.[35]

During the terrible persecution of Decius (250) many Catholics fell away either by openly and freely sacrificing to the gods
(*sacrificati quasi sponte*) or by doing so under violence (*sacrificati
sub violentia*). Finally there was the third category of those who
had obtained a false statement saying that they had done so
(*libellati*).

Cyprian was faced with a difficult situation, but he objected
to the many priests who were granting reconciliation to these
lapsi. In his absence, they were reconciling these lapsed without
penance, and what is worse, without permission of the bishop,
who alone can reconcile sinners: "I hear that some of the
presbyters are neither mindful of the gospel nor do they consider what the martyrs have written to me, nor do they reserve
to the bishop the honor of his priesthood and chair, but they
have already begun to communicate the lapsed and to give them
the Eucharist. Where it was proper they should have attained
all this through approved procedure."[36] Cyprian goes on to explain that the procedure is confession (*exomologesis*) followed
by penance and reconciliation. Even the recommendation of
those who suffered for the faith (the confessors) given to the
lapsed for their reconciliation was nothing more than a recommendation to the bishop. Final reconciliation is reserved to the
bishop alone. St. Cyprian says this: "and so direct letters (i.e.,
those of the confessors) to us in conformity with faith and
discipline."

He then awaited a general council of bishops who would
settle the matter. This council met at Carthage in 251, and
after reading Sacred Scripture favoring both forgiveness and se-

[35] M. Bevenot, "The Sacrament of Penance and St. Cyprian's De Lapsis,"
Theological Studies, 16 (1955), 189–196.
[36] Epistle 17 (*CSEL*, 3, 522).

verity, the council decided that (1) hope should never be taken away from any of the *lapsi*, (2) the *libellati* were to be reconciled immediately after a severe penance, (3) the *sacrificati* of both groups only at the hour of their death.[37] In 252, however, at the Second Council of Carthage, the question of doctrine, as such, was raised. Here there is no doubt that the Church of Africa maintained that *in principle* all sins — of whatever nature (*in hominem et in Deum*) were within the power of the keys of the Church. Reconciliation was promised to all the lapsed who would do penance. The proof adduced by the African bishops was the famous text of Mt 16:18: "Whatever you shall loose on earth shall be loosed in heaven. . . ."

The doctrine of St. Cyprian is therefore a further clarification and proof of the Church's power to reconcile and forgive sinners by virtue of the power given the bishops of the Catholic Church. Some Catholics as well as Protestants have claimed that this reconciliation was of a purely external nature, a reconciliation which had no real effect on the internal condition of the sinner. This notion, however, is in complete contradiction to all the evidence we have. For Tertullian this penance and reconciliation remitted even eternal punishment, and this is to say that it has a real internal effect. St. Cyprian argues again and again from the text of St. Matthew that what the bishops do on earth will be done in heaven and that, if they reconcile a sinner, so does God. This is axiomatic with St. Cyprian. "Nothing could be more paradoxical, for the whole Treatise (*De lapsis*) is to exhort those who had fallen from the Church in the persecution of Decius to submit to the penance expected of them by the Church, so that they might be reconciled by the Church through the imposition of the bishop's hands and then re-admitted to Holy Communion."[38] And again, in another work written directly against the Novatian heretics, *Ad Novatianum*, St. Cyprian says:

---

[37] Epistle 55 (*CSEL*, 3, 641 ff.). See also B. Poschmann, "Die Dogmatischen Veraussetzungen der Cyprianischen Busspraxis," in *Zeitschrift für Kath. Theologie*, 37 (1913), 244–265.

[38] M. Bevenot, art. cit., p. 175.

"For what has been justly refused in this life cannot be granted hereafter. For it is here, as the Lord has said, that sins are either bound or loosed; in the hereafter there will be nothing else but reward or condemnation. For everyone who is justly condemned here, cannot be numbered among the elect or be judged worthy of the life to come."[39]

Conclusion From This Period. It is clear that our evidence for the penitential discipline is not very extensive; but from what we have, we can deduce all the elements necessary for showing us that all the essentials are here present for the sacrament of penance.

1. The Church is composed of both saints and sinners. Nothing could be further from the truth than to say that sinners are excluded from its community. The invitation to penance in all of these documents we have examined presupposes this fact.

2. The Church has the power to forgive (reconcile) every type of sinner; moreover, in the tradition of the Church, no real evidence can be adduced to prove the contention of Tertullian that certain sins could not be forgiven. Adultery was reconciled in *The Shepherd of Hermas*; a murderer is reconciled in the story of Clement of Alexandria; and, finally, those who had apostatized from the faith are given hope of forgiveness in the texts of St. Cyprian.

3. Forgiveness by the Church is so powerful that it attains the internal guilt and sinful condition of the penitent. It was not simply an external absolution from ecclesiastical censures, but reconciliation with the Church that was recognized as reconciliation with God. The text which is habitually used is that of Mt 16:18.

4. This power of forgiveness is directly given to the bishops of the Church and not just to the Church in general. This was the Catholic doctrine as it is given indirectly by Tertullian in his attacks on the Catholic Church. This doctrine emerges even more clearly from St. Cyprian for whom this element of penance

---

[39] *Contra Novatianum* (*P.L.*, 35, c. 2305).

is axiomatic. This is such a reality for him that not even the pleas and recommendations of the confessors and martyrs were sufficient to forgive sin; their petitions must be presented to the bishop who alone can reconcile sinners to the Church.

5. Because of an increasingly rigorist attitude, the penitential discipline can be received but once in the Church and for this reason will become a great pastoral problem in later centuries. In reality, the problem will not be cleared up until the introduction of private penance by the Irish missionaries of the fifth and sixth centuries. Various councils such as that held at Elvira (305) will legislate in a more rigorist vein, but the doctrinal foundation remains clear. During the times of persecution, the temptation to apostatize was great; stern measures therefore had to be taken to strengthen the resolve of Christians. This policy toward sinners was, then, a matter of discipline and not of doctrine.

II. The Practice of Penance in St. Augustine

The clearest picture of ecclesiastical penance during this early patristic period is given by St. Augustine of Hippo (died 430).[40] His doctrine is spread through many of his writings, but it always remains essentially the same: The Church in the person of her bishop can and does reconcile sinners (of whatever nature) to herself and therefore with God. The power of the bishops is so great that whatever is done on earth will also be done in heaven.[41]

We find this doctrine of St. Augustine well illustrated in one of his epistles where he describes the different forms of penance in the Church (he calls them *actiones poenitentiae*).

---

[40] Palmer, *op. cit.*, pp. 96–109; P. Anciaux, *Le Sacrément de la Pénitence*, pp. 57–64; Latin texts collected in *Enchiridion Theologicum Sancti Augustini* (BAC, N. 205), pp. 620–626; K. Adam, *Die Kirchliche Sünden-vegebung Nach dem hl. Augustin*, pp. 17–26; F. Hunermann, *Die Busslehre des Heiligen Augustinus*, pp. 50–68.

[41] *Sermo* 351 (P.L., 38, c. 1535–1549) and *Sermo* 352 (P.L., 38, c. 1549–1560).

He first argues that there are three such forms of penance in Holy Scripture. Augustine then goes on to describe these various forms of penance in the Church:

1. The first form is that which is done before baptism (it must be remembered that it was customary in Augustine's day to baptize mostly adults[42] as a preparation for entrance into the Church. He tells us that, by this penance, sorrow is followed by joy, putting off the old man in order to enter into the new, thus following Christ's injunction: "Repent and be baptized, for the Kingdom is at hand." "Every man, in fact, who is free at the moment when this sacrament of the faithful is given, cannot enter a new life without repenting of his former existence."

2. The second type of penance is that which is done for our daily sins which, he says, even the bishops commit. And for that reason, we must all strike our breasts in the mea culpa of the Confiteor at daily Mass. Here, St. Augustine gives the traditional ways of expiating these sins: alms, good works, prayer, etc. "Is it not for this reason that each day we strike our breast? Is it not for this reason that even we bishops do this each day as we ascend the altar? It is thus that we do this as saying each day of our lives: Forgive us our trespasses."

3. The third and last type is the "canonical penance," i.e., a public penance which must be performed for grave sins against the Decalogue, which have inflicted a grave wound. "This penance is painful. The wound is grave, an adultery has been committed, perhaps a murder or sacrilege! The case is grave, the wound serious, dangerous, mortal but the doctor (God) is all powerful." St. Augustine goes on to say that in this case there are three essential parts of the canonical penance which must be performed by the penitent in union with the Church to obtain God's forgiveness.[43] These are:

---

[42] See Augustine's own Confessions, Bk. 4, Ch. 6; J. Jeremias, Infant Baptism in the First Four Centuries (London, 1959), pp. 24-42 and abundant bibliography therein.

[43] We may note even here the three essential notes present in the penance

a) *Confession.* The man must judge himself severely, and this constitutes a condemnation of his own sins. "In this judgment, the man ought to judge himself severely in order that, having judged himself, he will not be judged by God. . . . Man must create a tribunal against himself . . . which is the conscience that tells him his sins are his accuser. . . . He must fear because his sins have made him God's enemy."[44]

b) *Excommunication.* This accusation cannot remain interior and secret. It must become external in a public recognition of his sin. The penitent must voluntarily separate himself from the Eucharistic banquet of which he has rendered himself unworthy. This liturgical separation expresses and admits his separation from the community of the faithful. But this voluntary excommunication must be ratified by the hierarchy. This separation is necessary so that the penitent may come to the forgiveness of his sins and to the reconciliation with the Church and with God. This power of the bishops is founded on the promise given by Christ to the Apostles and their successors. Thus they, who have been placed over the sacraments (the bishops), alone are to reconcile the sinner to the Church and to God. The penitent must submit to their judgment to escape divine condemnation.

> He who is encompassed by the chains of sins so dangerous cannot hesitate or defer to have recourse to the power of the leaders of the Church, by whom he will be delivered on earth in order that they [his sins] be not held in heaven. . . . Thus after having brought against himself this condemnation let him present himself to the bishops, by whom is exercised in the Church the power of the keys. And beginning once again to become a submissive son, respectful of the place of the members of the community, he will accept the satisfaction determined by them who are the *prepositi sacramentorum.* . . .

This confession of sin did not have to be public, but the ex-

---

in St. Augustine and traditional in the Church: (1) the part of the sinner (2) the part of the Church — hierarchy and faithful, (3) the part of God in forgiveness.

[44] We see here the eschatological aspect of penance in the anticipated judgment of the penitent by himself — thereby escaping the definitive judgment by God on the last day.

piation itself always had a public character.[45] This is an important
element both in St. Augustine and in all the earlier tradition of
the penitential discipline. We speak of "public" and "private"
penance today. This terminology should be understood as it was
used by St. Augustine and in earlier texts which we have already
cited. The work of Father Galtier has been very helpful in clarify-
ing this terminology of the early Church. The terms "public" and
"private," as they apply to penance, refer to the element of
satisfaction. They do not refer to the confession of sins, for this
was always private, nor to the element of reconciliation, which
was probably public both in St. Augustine and in other representatives of early tradition. In the early centuries of the Church,
then, or up to the eighth century, satisfaction for sins and reconciliation to the Church and to God will always have a more or
less public character. The penitent was always free to announce
his sins in public — and we have cases on record where this was
done — but we also know that it was not required. In any case,
the essential power of the Church to reconcile sinners to herself
and, by that fact, to God, remains always the same. Whether
the Church saw fit to exercise this power in a public or in a
more "private" way really makes little difference to the essential
aspects of this power.

c) *Satisfaction.* The third stage is reached when confession
and excommunication are duly imposed by the bishop, placing
the penitent among the special class of the *ordo poenitentium*,
i.e., the group of those who were performing some penance imposed by the Church. "If his sin was not only a grave sin but a
public scandal for others, and if the bishop judged it would be
useful for the Church that he do penance publicly and perhaps
in view of everyone, let him accept that decision without hesita-

---

[45] Grotz, *Die Entwicklung des Busstufenwesens in der Vonicanischen
Kirche* (Freiburg-im-Br., 1955), p. 87. See also: Poschmann, "Die Kirchliche Vermittlung der Sündervergebung nach Augustinus," in *Zeitschrift für
Theo. Kath.*, 45 (1921), 498: "The sacramental effect of ecclesial forgiveness
is essentially the lifting of the excommunication from the sinner and his reincorporation into the grace-dispensing community of the Church."

tion in order not to add to his wounds, already dangerous and mortal, the infection of shame." As we have already mentioned, secret sins did not have to be publicly confessed or known unless they were already public or unless the bishop should determine otherwise for the good of the Church. In any case, whether the sin was public or private, the penitent had to have recourse to the bishop for his forgiveness and be submissive to his judgment. After having completed this penance, with the help of the whole community who prays for him and under the authority and conduct of the bishop, the penitent is reconciled with the community and readmitted to the Eucharistic banquet. Such is the end of this official penance, being consummated by this new intervention of the authority of the Church, the sign and guarantee of the penitent's reconciliation with God.

As did St. Cyprian, St. Augustine justified this power of the bishop to forgive and reconcile by the texts of Mt 16:18 and Jn 20:23. Here we find a description of the power of the keys given to the Apostles and their successors, the bishops. We must also note the part of the whole community in the forgiveness of sins. It was the bishop alone who reconciled, but it was the whole body of the faithful who was to pray for the whole ordo poenitentium.[46]

It is evident, then, from these texts of St. Augustine that, in his thought, reconciliation to the Church in the person of the bishop, with the faithful aiding by their prayers, was of itself reconciliation with God because "whatsoever you bind on earth shall be bound in heaven." In another epistle, St. Augustine said, "Therefore Christ said to the ministers of His Church: 'What you loose on earth will be loosed in heaven'; you by whom hands are imposed on penitents."[47] St. Augustine explicitly tells us that

---

[46] In many respects, this important aspect of ecclesial penance has not been underlined enough in modern preaching and teaching. We tend to think of "confession," "expiation" as purely private affairs, whereas in reality it is of the greatest importance that the faithful pray for all the sinners in the Church.

[47] G. Morini, *Miscellanea Augustiniana* (Romae, 1930), p. 358.

this was the common practice in all the churches — in omnibus
ecclesiis.[48]

The penance described for us by St. Augustine is very telling.
The sinner must accuse himself both before God and before the
Church in view of pardon from both. The excommunication
which is meted out to him is of a medicinal nature. It is intended to bring about his healing. It is imposed by the ecclesiastical authority and its end is to make the guilty man reflect on
and repent of his sins. St. Augustine quotes 1 Cor 5:2, where
St. Paul excommunicated the incestuous man in order that he
may return, healed, to the Christian flock. It should be pointed
out that this excommunication should not be confused with
the disciplinary excommunication, later developed, which was
used by the Church to punish serious external breaches of God's
law. In any case, the medicinal excommunication to which St.
Augustine refers is from the Eucharist in the sense of "not to go
to Communion" (ex-Communio). The penitent, fearing a final
separation from the Kingdom of heaven, was to separate himself
for a time from the Eucharistic table.[49]

Finally, the satisfaction imposed by the bishop takes on two
particular aspects. While performing satisfaction, the penitent
belongs to a special class in the Church called the ordo poenitentium (the order of penitents), the group performing penance
for their sins. It is a satisfaction which is imposed by the bishop
who has the power of the keys in the Church. This satisfaction
not only serves as a personal remedy, but also as an example to
others: "He has committed a sin which is not only grave for
himself but which also constitutes a source of scandal for others;
therefore if the bishop judges it useful or necessary to impose a
public penance on the guilty man, this latter should not refuse,

---

[48] Ep. 265 (P.L., 55, c. 108). For an even more direct text, cf. Contra
Crescenium Donat., II, 12, 16: "The City of God by receiving sinners
makes them innocent." Even Galtier has to admit that "There can be no
remission of sin except in and through the Church" as his judgment of St.
Augustine's thought. Cf. De Poenitentia, Tractatus Dogmatico — Historicus,
p. 132.
[49] P. Anciaux, op. cit., p. 88.

but perform the penance in order not to add a sin of false pride to an already grave situation."[50] It can never be known if a penitent will have enough courage to undergo a penance. It is a responsibility that is incumbent on the whole community as such, not just the penitent. The fraternal element of the community of the Mystical Body is thus beautifully brought out in these communal prayers for sinners. Reconciliation accomplished by the bishop in the Church is also reconciliation with God.

Reconciliation with God, the complete cure of a man's sin, is attained by submission to ecclesial penance. The reconciliation with the Church is the efficacious sign of the peace and gift of the Holy Spirit, who reestablishes the gifts of baptism which were lost by sin. The accent, then, was put on the importance and the necessity of this submission to the official penance of the Church.[51]

With St. Augustine, then, we have a complete synthesis of penance in the early Church. In it, we see all the elements of the power of the Church to reconcile sinners to itself and, by that very fact, with God Himself. The evolution of the sacrament of penance has reached its clearest evolution in the description given us by St. Augustine of Hippo. With his witness, we may be permitted to conclude our study of penance in the early patristic period.

III. History of Penance During the Fifth and Sixth Centuries

We have seen that one of the chief characteristics of penance during the first four centuries was its unicity, or the fact that

---

[50] *Sermo* 351 (*P.L.*, 39, c. 1536–1538).

[51] St. Augustine describes the dangerous plight of those who are bound (*ligati*) in sin. When the Vandals were attacking Africa, St. Augustine urges the ministers of the Church to remain at their posts so as to be able to reconcile sinners and the dying. Otherwise — and Augustine is very explicit — they will be in danger of eternal damnation unless they are reconciled. To be reconciled therefore is to escape this eternal damnation. See *Epistle* 228, 8 (*P.L.*, 33, c. 1016).

public penance could be performed but once. To the list of authors already mentioned we may add the witness of Origen and St. Ambrose, who attest to this practice in both the Eastern and Western Churches. This aspect of penance was to pose a very grave pastoral problem in the fifth and sixth centuries.[52] This problem certainly came to the attention of the earlier Fathers, but we have already seen that, because of the difficult times of persecution, they favored a more rigorous approach. Yet, even during this early period we have various witnesses of clemency and mercy. As a matter of fact, the great doctor of the Church, St. John Chrysostom (408), introduced a new policy of mercy and clemency toward all sinners, even to those who had sinned after the first penance was performed: ". . . If you are a fornicator, or an adulterer, if you are an extortioner or greedy, come to the Church that you may learn to do these things no more . . . this I tell you every day. Come and be healed along with me. For I, too, the physician, have need of medicaments."[53] Yet, this policy of the great Doctor earned him many enemies and the irregular synod held at Chalcedon deposed him for this policy: "Seventh, that he holds out pardon for sinners by teaching the following: If you shall sin a second time, do penance a second time, and as often as you shall sin, come to me, and I shall cure you."[54] Chrysostom's policy was an innovation of mercy, and it will grow stronger as the Church realizes the almost impossibility of a policy of severity with respect to penance. This same attitude of mercy and clemency is even seen in some pontifical documents from Rome. The most outstanding witness here is that of Pope Innocent I. He is still in the tradition of one penance, but he says that all sinners, no matter who they are, should be reconciled, if they so request, at the hour of their death. Thus the status of the recidivist would preclude a second public penance and open fellowship with the community,

---

[52] Palmer, op. cit., pp. 123–171; Anciaux, op. cit., 65–93; B. Poschmann, Die Abendlandische Kirchenbusse in Früher Mittelalter, pp. 63–108.
[53] On the Incomprehensible Nature of God, homily 5, 6 (P.G., 48, c. 746).
[54] The Synod of the Oak (Mansi, III, c. 1146).

but would not deprive him of reconciliation and Viaticum at the approach of death:

> Now we have been asked what practice should be followed in the case of those who at the hour of death beg for penance and reconciliation of communion as well, even though from the time of their baptism and through the whole of life they have given themselves over to the pleasures of incontinency. With regard to such, the former discipline was rather harsh; but mercy intervened to make subsequent practice more lenient. . . . In view of the frequent persecution of those days, communion was withheld and for a good reason: readiness to grant communion would hardly deter from apostasy those who were assured of reconciliation. . . . But after the Lord had restored peace to His Churches and all cause for alarm was removed, it was decided to grant Communion to the dying. . . . Otherwise we might seem to follow the heretic Novatian in harsh and severe denial of pardon. Therefore along with penance, Communion (i.e., reconciliation) will be granted at the end, so that men of this sort, Our Savior willing, may be delivered from eternal destruction.[55]

Therefore, the tendency toward mercy was on the increase, but in general the harsh measures of the unique penance were still in vogue through the early Middle Ages. This became the general rule in the West and became known as the official canonical penance.[56] Varied arguments will be used to defend it doctrinally, such as the statement that just as there is but one baptism, so there can be but one penance. Thus penance was put off until the end of life, and it came to be looked on as a direct preparation for death rather than a destruction of sin during life.

A second factor and difficulty was the severe penance that was imposed on the penitent. Normal punishment forbade the penitent to bear arms and prevented him from carrying on a normal married life with his wife. Exile was sometimes imposed in the case of very serious crimes. Some Councils even discouraged the young from performing penance for fear of relapse and subsequent unreconciliation with the Church. St. Ambrose tells us

---

[55] Ep. 6; *To Exsuperies*, 2 (*P.L.*, 20, c. 498).
[56] Anciaux, *op. cit.*, p. 71.

that it was not wise to council a young man to do penance until his passions had subsided.[57] These penances remained in vigor even after a Christian had performed his official penance as guarantees that he would persevere in his repentant state until death. Thus the penitential life came to be looked upon more and more as a type of monastic life where penitents lived exactly as monks for the rest of their lives. It is due to these arduous demands that penance became a direct preparation for death during the fifth through the eighth centuries.

Another preparation for private penance was the fact that neither clerics nor religious could do public penance.[58] This does not mean that ecclesiastical discipline was not severe for them; on the contrary, a cleric who fell into serious sin was considered a recidivist and was put on the same level as the Christian who had done penance but had fallen again. Normally, both these classes of sinners could be reconciled only at the hour of death. Often, too, sinful clerics were forced to become monks with the result that the monastic state was considered a penitential state. The result, in general, was that a very important segment of the community was excluded from public penance and therefore from reconciliation with the Church.

All these circumstances created a very difficult pastoral problem for the Church. "In Poschmann's view it is the absence of a private penance — even for lesser sins — that led to the complete decadence of morals in the late fifth and sixth centuries and to an almost complete abandonment of the sacrament as the ordinary redeeming for sin to be made use of at the time of death. Thus, Poschmann brings his work to a close with what appears to be a veiled censure of the Church's inability to direct the moral life of her children. . . ."[59] It would seem, from a purely

---

[57] See, for example, the decree of the local Council of Agde in 506. ". . . penance is not to be granted readily to young people on account of the inconstancy of youth" (*Mansi*, VIII, c. 327).

[58] In the words of Pope St. Leo I: "It is foreign to Church practice that those who have been consecrated to the priestly dignity . . . should receive an imposition of the hand as the remedy or penance for some crime of theirs." Epis. 167, *To Rusticus* (*P.L.*, 54, c. 1203).

[59] P. Palmer, op. cit., p. 356.

objective study of the texts of this period, that Poschmann's point of view is quite correct. In the form of penance then in existence, a whole mass of Christians was left to its own resources: clerics and religious who had sinned grievously, recidivists of all types, and a great number of ordinary Christians who feared the rigors of the penitential discipline, could only obtain their reconciliation at the hour of death.

In certain regions, however, we find a certain number of individual churches which were reconciling sinners after the fashion of St. John Chrysostom who, as we have seen, welcomed sinners who had sinned more than once. In these churches, sinners, even recidivists, were received after the performance of even private penitential practices as well as through simple amelioration of their sinful lives. Once again, however, we note a violent reaction and condemnation of these individual practices by various councils in the Church. The Third Council of Toledo in 589 declared that "We have come to learn that in certain Spanish Churches men do penance for their sins not in accord with canonical precedent (i.e., the unicity of penance) but in a most offensive manner, namely, as often as they are pleased to sin, so often they demand of the presbyter to be reconciled. Accordingly, to suppress a presumption so horrible the holy Council commands that penances be assigned according to the form of the ancient canon."[60]

These elements of "private penance" which were developing in this period, and which certain churches substituted for the rigorous public penance, pose a problem for Catholic scholars. There is little agreement among them about the evolution of private penance. According to Galtier and Adam there was an official form of private penance in existence in the Church from the very earliest times along with the official canonical and public penance. The existence of such a private penitential discipline is denied by such eminent scholars as Poschmann and K. Rahner.[61] They state that these exceptional forms of penance

---

[60] Third Council of Toledo (589) in *Mansi*, IC, c. 995.
[61] P. Galtier, *L'Eglise et la Rémission des Péchés*, p. 209; B. Poschmann,

were never recognized or ratified by a general liturgical rite.
According to these authors, private penance was generally considered as an abuse and was treated as such. What the texts do
allow us to state with certainty, however, is that this private form
of penance will become more and more popular, and finally it
will win official ecclesiastical recognition alongside the official
canonical and public penance. This will be the matter of the
next chapter. For the present, it is enough to say that during
this whole period of the fifth and sixth centuries, canonical
penance alone was recognized as official in the Church. In practice, however, this penance was restricted to a very small number of Christians because of the rigors involved. It was considered as a direct preparation for death, not as the ordinary
remedy for sin during life. These and other odious demands of
the penitential discipline made penance objectionable for the
great majority of Christians. From a pastoral point of view, the
situation was extremely confusing and inefficacious. It is with
these perspectives in mind that we can better understand the
innovations of the seventh and eighth centuries.[62]

IV. History of Penance From the Seventh
to the Tenth Centuries

This is a period of change. The principal actors of this period
were the Irish monks who came to the Continent to preach and
teach during the seventh and eighth centuries. It is to them, more
than to any others, that we owe the practice of the more private
type of the penitential discipline.

The situation of the Church in the Celtic and Irish Churches
was quite different from those on the Continent.[63] In sixth-

---

in *Theolog. Quartalschrift*, 114 (1933), 149–156. For reference to all these
authors and their respective arguments, see B. Poschmann, *Die Abendlandische Kirchenbusse im Ausgang des Christlichen Altertums*, pp. 205–
211.

[62] P. Anciaux, *op. cit.*, p. 80.

[63] John Ryan, *Irish Monasticism — Origins and Early Development* (Dublin, 1931), pp. 340–361.

century Ireland, due to the absence of large cities, the Church was monastic in character, and the religious life of the people was therefore centered around the abbot and his monks. It is clear, then, that the abbot was the spiritual father of both his monks and the people of the surrounding regions as well. Furthermore, being at a distance from the Continent itself, the practice of canonical penance had not been introduced into these regions.[64] Penance was administered in a more private fashion as well as the satisfaction and "reconciliation with the altar," as it was called by these Irish monks. It was the priest-monk who heard confessions of penitents and reconciled them as well. This then was the practice, of necessity, in the Irish and Celtic Church of the sixth through the ninth centuries.

This, of course, is not to say that these Celtic and Irish practices were less rigorous, and even, at times, less public than penance done on the Continent. If we read the various penitentials of this period (v.g., of *Finnian* and *Columban*) we will see quite the contrary.[65] The disabilities and disqualifications visited upon penitents by these monks were often quite vigorous. For the more serious crimes, for example, long pilgrimages and sometimes even exile itself was enjoined. "It is, therefore, a bit tendentious to discover in the Celtic discipline a spirit of humaneness and understanding that was wanting to the rest of the Church during the first seven centuries."[66]

Yet, the essential and most important element of the form of penance introduced by these monks was the elimination of the more awesome features of public and canonical penance. Carrying arms, conducting business, having a normal married life after penance were all taken for granted by the monks. Above all, private penance could be received more than once, and thus a great pastoral problem was removed from the Church with

[64] R. C. Mortimer, *Origins of Private Penance in the Western Church* (Oxford, 1939), p. 136.
[65] For a list of the various Irish and Celtic penitentials see the non-Catholic study of J. T. McNeill and H. M. Gamer, *Medieval Handbooks of Penance* (New York, 1938).
[66] P. Palmer, art. cit., p. 339.

one stroke. If we remember that canonical penance could be given but once and that this was put off more or less until the time of death, we shall realize what an advantage this form of private penance really was for Christians, especially recidivists. Again, even clerics and religious could undergo such a form of penance because of the nonpublic element inherent in it. From a purely pastoral point of view, it made the sacrament less odious to a large segment of Christian people and it responded to a real need in the community. This explains why private penance will become more and more widespread throughout the Christian world, and later will be given an equal footing with the canonical penance. The Latin adage during the later period of the eighth century became: *Peccata privata, poenitentia privata; Peccata publica, poenitentia publica.* As a matter of fact, so popular and widespread had this private form of penance become that toward the end of the ninth century, public, canonical penance exists in name only.

The introduction of private penance did not go unchallenged. Various reactions can be noted on the Continent, especially in Spain. We have already seen the reaction of the Third Council of Toledo in 589 against those who dared to reconcile the sinner more than once. Objection continued in the Spanish Church until the Council of Chalon in 813. The churches of Gaul, on the other hand, went along quite well with this new type of penance introduced by the Irish monks. Some bishops at the Council of Chalon tried to reintroduce the earlier practice of public and canonical penance but recognized that they were attempting to reverse a *fait accompli*: "The performance of penance according to the ancient institution of the Canons has in many localities lapsed into disuse, and neither is the order of the ancient custom of reconciliation observed: Let the help of the Lord Emperor be sought, that if anyone sins publicly, he may be punished with public penance and, in accord with canonical procedure, he may be excommunicated and reconciled according to his deserts" (Canon 25).[67] The Council of Rheims held dur-

---

[67] See *Mansi*, XIV, c. 98–100.

ing this period is even more explicit. It urges that "discrimination be observed between penitents: Who should do penance publicly and who secretly" (Canon 31).

To aid the monk-priests in administering the sacrament of penance, various penitential books (*libri poenitentiales*) were composed by unknown authors. They listed the various sins and the corresponding punishments (penance) to be given to the penitent. These books are at the origin of our present-day "confessor guides" which aid the confessor in the equitable distribution of penance for various offenses. Among the various penitentials in use by the Irish and Celtic monks, we note those of Columban (600), Finnian (550), and Theodore (690). There was a violent reaction against them at the Council of Chalon, which claimed that the authors were uncertain, but certain were the errors. But, in general, their use continued to aid the confessor-priest until the late Middle Ages.[68]

Another feature of the greatest importance in this evolution of the sacrament toward a more private form is the fact that all the main and essential factors found in the earlier penitential procedure are also found in private penance.[69] In other words, even though the sacrament was administered privately, the ecclesial element was still present. Formerly, penance was conducted by the intervention and authority of the Church in virtue of the power of the keys; this same element was clearly affirmed in this newly evolved form of penitential administration. The expiation for sin was done in union with the Church and under her authority, for outside the Church there was no forgiveness of sin. In this evolved form of private penance there was the complete and detailed confession of all serious sins committed after baptism. The thirty-second canon of the Council of Chalon made this very clear: "But we have discovered that the following is also in need of correction, that some when they confess their sins to the priests do not do so in full. . . . Accordingly, let one

---

[68] R. C. Mortimer, *op. cit.*, p. 108; O. D. Watkins, *History of Penance*, II, pp. 120–153.
[69] P. Anciaux, *op. cit.*, pp. 84–85.

who confesses his sins be instructed to make confession concerning the eight principal vices. . . ." In other words, all serious sins had to be confessed. The initiative of such a confession was in the hands of the sinner, and if he wished to receive pardon, he had to approach the priest and confess all his serious sins.

The Church was again present in her duly appointed minister, the priest who accepted the confession of the penitent in the name of the Church.[70] It was he who now judged the sincerity of the penitent and imposed the penance. At first the reconciliation or absolution was given only after the penance was actually performed, but with the passage of time, it became more and more customary to give it before the penance had been actually completed, provided there was a firm intention of fulfilling the penance imposed by the priest. Finally, in 1215, the Fourth Council of the Lateran decreed that the faithful had to confess all their mortal sins at least once a year in order to receive the paschal Communion. Before this time, the initiative of penance was left entirely to the penitent in view of expiation of his sins.

A final element ought to be added in this discussion of private penance. Besides the expiation and destruction of sin which was brought about by the collaboration of the penitent and the exercise of the keys in confession, confession was also considered as therapeutic.[71] The confession of faults takes on the aspect of a humiliation which is in itself the beginning of the expiation of sin. The confessor had to know each sin committed, not only in order to impose a proportional penance, but also in order to know the spiritual condition of his penitent. "Spiritual direction" was first introduced as early as the time of Origen in a nonsacramental confession of faults by the monks of a monastery. The individual monks in the monastery were encouraged to discuss and reveal their faults with a spiritual father who was not necessarily a priest. With the introduction of private penance, the therapeutic element with its emphasis on "helping the peni-

---

[70] J. Leclercq, "La Sainte Eglise et la remission des Péchés," in *l'Eglise et le Pécheur*, p. 20.

[71] Battifol, *Etudes d'Histoire Positive*, I (Paris, 1927), pp. 189–210.

tent" by encouragement and advice became more and more important in the administration of the sacrament of penance.

Conclusion

Let us conclude our rather brief analysis of the sacrament of penance. The sacrament of ecclesial penance to which is attached full reconciliation with God is an undeniable reality in the history of the Church. We have seen that the external form of this sacrament has undergone considerable evolution during the passage of the centuries from a public and external penance to the more private type with which we are familiar today. However, the internal and essential structure and constitution of the reality of penance remains the same today as it did 1900 years ago. We have shown that the significance of this sacrament has remained essentially unchanged: a process wherein God, the sinner, and the Church each cooperate for the destruction of sin and reconciliation with the Church and, through her, with God. Each has an essential part to play in the destruction of sin; if any one of the three elements — God, the sinner, or the Church — is taken away, there can be no forgiveness of sin. It is this that the Fathers and the early Church always considered the reality of penance.

CHAPTER VII

The Church and Forgiveness of Sin

INTRODUCTION

This chapter is added because of the increasing interest of theologians in the relationship between the forgiveness of sin and the Church. For the first ten centuries, the sacrament of penance was a reality in the Church, conducted and directed under her authority in virtue of the promise of Christ to the Apostles and, through them, to the bishops, that "whatsoever you shall loose on earth shall be loosed also in heaven" (Mt 16:18). For the Fathers there could be no reconciliation or forgiveness of sin outside the visible institution which is the Church.[1] Only Tertullian, the Montanist, denied that the Church in the person of her bishops had received this power to bind and to loose. He said, in effect, that "the decision [to forgive sin] belongs to the Lord, and not to the servant, to God Himself, and not to the priest." In interpreting the famous text of Mt 16:18 he said that Christ indeed gave the full power of forgiveness to the Apostles but not to the bishops, their successors. In other words, for Tertullian this gift was a personal one intended only for the Apostles. Tertullian, however, stands alone in thus interpreting this famous text. In the twelfth century Peter Abelard returned to this interpretation, but he finally renounced it.[2] In any case, for the Fathers, reconciliation of the sinner with God

---

[1] See B. Leeming, *Principles of Sacramental Theology* (Westminster, Md., 1954), pp. 252–261; M. J. Scheeben, *The Mysteries of Christianity* (St. Louis, 1958), pp. 570–585; M. Schmaus, *Katholische Dogmatik*, IV, I (München), pp. 614–635; A. d'Ales, "La Pénitence," in *Recherches de Science Religieuse*, 12 (1922), 372–380.

[2] See his famous text in his *Ethics* (*P.L.*, 178, c. 672–674) and his consequent retraction cited in P. Anciaux, *La Théologie du Sacrément de Pénitence au XII* Siècle*, p. 290.

was possible only in and through the Church. Her powers were so great that what she did on earth was also done in heaven.

The relationship between the sinner, the Church, and God was never put into technical language by the Fathers themselves. This was to be the work of the scholastic theologians of the twelfth century through their teaching on the *res*, the *sacramentum tantum*, and the *res et sacramentum*. Although a detailed examination of this period is beyond the scope of this work, the essential feature of this scholastic tradition can be seen by observing that, by *res et sacramentum*, the scholastic theologians understood the symbolic reality which is both the immediate effect of the sacramental rite (*sacramentum tantum*) and the sign, pledge, or disposition for the ultimate effect of the sacrament which is sacramental grace (*res tantum*). Nevertheless, the scholastic period, because of a lack of historical perspective, did not develop the element of the relationship between the Church and the sinner. Certainly, the essential elements remained. The Church in the person of her bishop had the power of the keys, and confession had to be made to the bishop and the penance imposed by the Church had to be fulfilled in order for the sinner to obtain forgiveness of his sins and reconciliation with God. Yet, it remains true to say that, during the scholastic period, the ecclesial element does not appear with the same clarity as it did in the earlier patristic period of the Church when the public and ecclesial character of penance was so strongly emphasized: the excommunication by the bishop, the *ordo poenitentium*, the prayers of the whole community for this class of sinners, the reconciliation by the bishop on the appointed day after the completion of the penance, all served to show the fundamental efficacy of ecclesial penance as a reality within and under the authority of the Church.

I. HISTORICAL PERSPECTIVE

Theologians of the past 100 years have once again made a great effort to point out the ecclesial and communal aspect of sin and its forgiveness in the body of the Church. Historical studies of the first centuries of the Church have served to show how really fundamental this relationship was and continues to be. This has come about principally by a double action and line of thought on the part of modern theologians: (1) a more profound and accurate historical research into the practice of penance in the early Church and (2) theological studies on the mystery of the Church Herself.[3] To quote one of these theologians: "Grace does not set up a purely individual relationship between the soul and God or Christ; rather, each one receives grace in the measure in which he is joined socially to that unique organism in which there flows its own life-giving stream. . . . All the sacraments are essentially 'Sacraments in the Church'; in her alone they produce their full effect, for in her alone, 'the Society of the Spirit,' is there, normally speaking, a sharing in the gift of the spirit."[4] There is no salvation, no forgiveness of sin outside of the ecclesial body. The *virtue of penance of the penitent* is united with the life-giving *virtue of the passion of Christ* only in the Church through her qualified ministers who have been entrusted with the keys.[5] Thus St. Thomas was able to write: "There is no true contrition [and therefore forgiveness of sin] without the intention of confessing."[6] There is no reconciliation with God without the will to do penance, i.e., without submitting to ecclesial penance, which is confession. This aspect of penance, as forgiveness in the Church, was made strikingly evident in the expert historical analyses of B. Poschmann[7] and B. Xiberta.[8] Xiberta's thesis is that reconciliation with the Church is the *res*

---

[3] P. Anciaux, *Le Sacrément de la Pénitence*, p. 193; H. De Lubac, *Catholicism*, 1954, pp. 35–50; Congar, *Esquisses du mystère de l'Eglise*, 1953, pp. 64–78; E. Mersch, *La Théologie du Corps Mystique*, 1944, pp. 60–75; Xiberta, *Clavis Ecclesiae*, 1922, pp. 9–12; P. Palmer, "The Theology of the Res et Sacramentum with particular emphasis on its application to penance," in *Proceedings of CTSA*, 1959, p. 121.

[4] H. De Lubac, op. cit., pp. 57–58.

[5] St. Augustine, *Sermo* 351 (*P.L.*, 38, c. 1535–1549).

[6] St. Thomas, *Comm. in IV Sent.*, D. 17, 2. 5. 2 ad 1; 3. 1. 4; 3. 5. 1.

[7] *Poenitentia Secunda*, 1950; *Die Busse*, 1951.

[8] *Clavis Ecclesiae* (Rome, 1922).

et sacramentum,[9] i.e., that reconciliation with the Church is the infallible sign leading to and indicating something further, God's forgiveness. This thesis has now become an accepted theory among Catholic theologians.[10]

Many of the texts of the Fathers have been cited in this study of the history of penance during the first eight centuries. Not cited, however, is an outstanding passage of the great Eastern doctor of the Church, St. Ephrem (c. A.D. 360), which Father Palmer cites in one of his articles on penance and which is reproduced here:

> Our Lord strengthened His Apostles with the grace that He had prayed for, gladdened their hearts, and after expressing peace unto them, He joyfully addressed them: "As the Father sent me . . . so do I, whom you here see, now send you; receive from me the Holy Spirit, that you may be filled with the Spirit and the power of forgiving them their sins, for whose sins you shall forgive, I shall forgive unto him, and whose sins you shall retain, they shall be retained by me (Jn 20:23). Moreover, what you shall loose or retain, so shall it be in heaven, nor will I gainsay your words, but in the Spirit, speak what is just. Receive a power which will neither leave you nor fail, because your word is guaranteed. Your words I shall not undo: If you shall be angry, I too will be angry; if you shall be reconciled [to the sinner], I will be reconciled. Behold I hang at your sides the keys of the Kingdom. Open and close it with fairness until I shall come in glory."[11]

St. Leo the Great, in one of his famous texts,[12] continues this same tradition that forgiveness of sin only comes through and by the Church. Cyprian, Augustine, and even Tertullian believed this, and Pope St. Leo only continues it when he says:

> The manifold mercy of God has come to the rescue of men in their repeated falls, that not only through the grace of baptism, but through the medicine of penance as well, hope of eternal life

---

[9] B. Leeming, *Principles of Sacramental Theology*, pp. 263–265.

[10] Palmer, *art. cit.*, p. 135. Palmer cites such eminent theologians as Poschmann, K. Rahner, Amann, Schmaus, De Lubac, and Leeming, and their appropriate bibliographies.

[11] Sermon for the Nocturn of the Lord's Resurrection (ed. by Lamy, I, 550 ff.).

[12] D.B. 146, 147, Mansi, VI, 209A, Ep. 108 (*P.L.*, 54, 101 f.).

is restored; with the result that those who have despoiled themselves of the gift of regeneration, by passing their own sentence of condemnation against themselves, have attained the forgiveness of their crimes. These remedies of divine goodness have been so arranged that God's pardon cannot be gained except through the supplication of the priests. For the mediator of God and men, the man Jesus Christ, has passed on this power to these who are placed over the Church, that they may grant both the discipline of penance to those who confess and, after they have been cleansed by salutary satisfaction, they may admit the same through the door of reconciliation to fellowship in the Sacraments. (Cf. D.B. 146, 147.)

The text could not be clearer. There is no reconciliation with God outside of the Church, and forgiveness of sins is reserved to the priests so that their judgment is God's judgment.

There are a multitude of other texts cited by Xiberta which could serve the same purpose, but to multiply them here would not be fitting.[13] The entire patristic period established quite clearly the fact of penance as an institution; it was definitely understood as essentially ecclesial, i.e., forgiveness of any grievous sin was to be submitted to the Church in the form of her hierarchy which has been appointed by Christ for this work. Reconciliation with the Church was reconciliation with God, and there was no forgiveness outside of the Church. In the words once again of St. Leo the Great:

But if anyone of those for whom we make supplication shall be prevented by some obstacle and lose the gift of present pardon, and before he receives the prescribed remedies, shall, in accord with the lot of men, finish his mortal life, what he did not receive while in the body, he shall not be able to gain when he has put off the flesh. . . . In this way, he wills that his own power shall strike us with dread and that fear of this sort shall be

---

[13] St. John Chrysostom, De Sacerdotio, III, 5; text of St. Innocent I, Ep. 6 (P.L., 20, 498); St. Siricius, Ad Himerium, 5 (P.L., 13, 1137); St. Jerome, Commentarium in Mathaeum, 16:19 (P.L., 26, 122); St. Pacian, Epistola ad Sympreniam, 1 (P.L., 13, 1057); Exortatio ad poenitentiam, (P.L., 13, 1085); St. Ambrose, On the Holy Spirit (P.L., 16, 755); St. Cyril of Alexandria, Commentarium in Joannem, 20:23 (P.G., 74, 721); St. Athanasius, Fragmentum (P.G., 26, 1316). Many places of Eusebius' Ecclesiastical History (P.G., 67, 1457; 68, 614); St. Basil the Great, To Amphilechius (P.G., 32, 728).

profitable to all, and that no one shall fail to dread the lot of certain ones who have been indifferent and negligent. For it is highly useful and necessary that the guilt of sins be loosed *by priestly supplication* before the last day. . . .[14]

St. Leo, then, is very clear in saying that one who dies without this reconciliation by priestly ministry (the Church) must indeed be afraid, for if his sin is not forgiven by the Church while he is alive, it shall not be so when he dies. Actually this is just another way of phrasing Mt 16:18: "What you shall bind on earth, etc."

Xiberta argues convincingly from all these primitive texts to the conclusion that reconciliation with the Church is the sign and the assurance of a further effect, God's forgiveness of the sinner, i.e., the *res et sacramentum* of the sacrament of penance.[15] Poschmann, considered one of the greatest experts in the field, agrees fully with him as do most theologians today. Summing up the whole question of the Church's power to forgive sin, he poses the following questions: Can the Church forgive sins which God wishes to forgive? Does God wish to forgive sins after a long penance? The Fathers unanimously answer affirmatively to the first question. We could easily give abundant evidence for this from St. Cyprian and other Church Fathers.[16] Arguing convincingly on almost every text of the Fathers, Poschmann shows that this reconciliation with the Church is (1) a true sacramental effect, for it is the remedy of sin, is (2) the help of the dying and their peace, is (3) the cause of their very salvation, and (4) that the dying must hold on to the "peace of the Church" at all costs, for to lose it is to lose eternal life.[17] Several factors contributed to the fact that this notion was not brought out better during the past 1000 years: (1) the more private performance of penance from the seventh century onward in which reconciliation of the Church, although present cer-

---

[14] Ep. 108, 4 (*P.L.*, 54, 101 f.).
[15] Xiberta, *op. cit.*, pp. 28, 30, 42–43, 45, 47–48, 51, 58–59, etc.
[16] *Ibid.*, p. 45.
[17] See in particular the letter of the Roman clergy to the clergy of Carthage, Epistle 8 (*CSEL*, 3, 485–487).

tainly in the qualified minister representing the Church, still was
not seen as clearly as the public penance and reconciliation of
the first centuries;[18] (2) the notion, introduced by Scotus, of the
"two ways" of forgiving sins, a theory which was as destructive
of the ecclesial character of penance as it was of all tradition in
the Church with regard to the sacrament of penance;[19] (3) the
more or less juridicial notion of the mystery of the Church which
has come down from the Middle Ages, through the Reforma-
tion, to our own day.[20] Yet there is today a revival of theological
thought of the interior and mystical aspect of the Church and its
interdependence on external structure.[21] What contemporary
research into the mystery of the Church shows is this: the
Church is the sanctifying fullness of Christians. In keeping with
the Pauline formula, theologians conclude that the Church is
the Body of Christ, His fullness or plerôma, that is to say, the
sphere in which is exercised the power of life and sanctification
of Him who fulfills holiness completely in all (cf. Eph 1:23).[22]

18 Anciaux, op. cit., p. 44.
19 H. Dondaine, l'Attrition Suffisante (Paris, 1943), pp. 16–26.
20 Jean Leclercq, Jean de Paris et l'Ecclésiologie du XIIIᵉ Siècle (Paris,
1942); G. de Lagarde, La Naissance de l'Esprit laique (Louvain, 1954), 6 v;
A. Fiske, La Reform Gregorienne (Louvain, 1943); P. S. Jaki, Les Tend-
ences Nouvelles de l'Ecclésiologie (Roma, 1957), pp. 5–17; Y. Congar,
"Affirmation de l'Autorité," in l'Écclesiologie au XIXᵉ Siècle (Paris, 1960),
pp. 77–114.
21 For abundant bibliography, cf. Jaki, op. cit., 8–54; Y. Congar,
Esquisses du Mystere de l'Eglise, 1953; E. Mersch, The Theology of the
Mystical Body, 1954; H. De Lubac, Catholicism, pp. 17–34; The Splendour
of the Church, 1956; L. Cerfaux, The Church in the Theology of St. Paul,
1959; S. Tromp, Corpus Christi quod est Ecclesia, 1960; G. Thils, Orienta-
tiens de la Théologie, 1958.
22 Cf. Cerfaux, op. cit., p. 323. Father Huby, in commenting on this
passage of the Epistle to the Ephesians says: "The Church is the 'pleroma'
of Christ, because she is the perfect receptacle for His graces and gifts;
she is completely filled by them, and in her they radiate their divine
energies." Saint Paul, Epîtres de la Capitivité (Paris, 1935), p. 169.
It was the same argument that the Fathers used: "The remission of sins,
since it cannot be granted except in the Holy Spirit is granted only in that
Church which has the Holy Spirit. For 'outside this body the Holy Spirit
vivifies no one.' And again: 'The Charity of the Church which is poured
out into our hearts forgives the sins of those who are members of the
Church, but it retains the sins of those who are not her members.'" Cf.
St. Augustine, Sermo 71, 20, 23; Ep. 185, 50; In Joan., Tr. 121, 4.

In the conception of St. Paul, there can be no divine life outside the sphere of the Church since she is Christ's plerôma or fulfillment. In some way, all must be saved through her; *Extra Ecclesiam nulla salus.*[23] And since the divine life is exercised only in her, she is the necessary earthly means for obtaining the Kingdom of which she is the beginning (baptism) and for forgiveness of sin for those who have fallen from their baptismal purity (penance). As the Council of Trent teaches, these two sacraments are intimately related to each other, the latter being "the second refuge after shipwreck."[24] Thus we can truly say, "*Extra Ecclesiam nulla remissio peccatorum.*" The Council of Trent and St. Thomas (who united the three elements of penance: the acts of the penitent [*virtus poenitentiae*], the power of the keys of the Church [*potestas clavium*], and the forgiveness of God [*remissio peccatorum*])[25] taught that it is only by this sacrament or its desire that sins are forgiven. The sacrament of penance, both in tradition and in theology, becomes essentially an ecclesial reality.[26]

---

[23] *Mystici Corporis Christi* of Pius XII clearly teaches this as did all tradition before him. Cf. *AAS*, 35 (1943), 220–275. It is interesting also to observe how His Holiness condemns the doctrine which would make a split or distinction between the visible and invisible Church. They are two parts of the same vital organism and can in no way be separated. They are distinct but intimately united. This doctrine is especially apropos to the theology of the sacrament of penance: the invisible element in the Church, the divine life of Christ in the faithful in the Holy Spirit who is the soul of the Church cannot be separated from the visible hierarchy who hold the power of the keys. Since they are inseparably united, it would be unthinkable to participate in the goods of the Spirit without due submission to and reconciliation with the visible Church in the ministry of penance. Cf. P. Riga, "The Ecclesiology of J. A. Möhler," *Theological Studies*, 22 (December, 1961), 563–587.

[24] D.B. 912.

[25] III, q. 85, art. 5 ad 2; IV Sent., d. 17, q. 2, a. 5; De Verit., q. 24, a. 15; III, q. 90, art. 2; III, q. 68, a. 4, ad 2; III, q. 84, a. 5, ad 2, etc.

[26] Sess. XIV, Ch. IV (D.B. 982) as quoted in Schroeder, *op. cit.*, p. 92; "The Council teaches, furthermore, that though it happens sometimes that this contrition is perfect through charity and reconciles man to God before this sacrament is actually received, this reconciliation, nevertheless, is not to be ascribed to the contrition itself without a desire of the sacrament, which desire is included in it."

St. Thomas was hampered, as were all the scholastics of his time, by a lack of historic perspective. This was, as we have said, one of the main reasons why most of the authors of the twelfth century and Duns Scotus in the late thirteenth had so many difficulties reconciling the acts of the penitent with the acts of the priest. This will also be the cause of the pseudo problems of the contritionists and attritionists of the sixteenth and seventeenth centuries; these pseudo problems resulted at times in some heated debates. If these authors had been more aware of the traditional notions on the sacramentality of penance, such discussions would have been, to a large degree, impossible. The problem was posed in false perspectives, especially by Duns Scotus and his "two ways" in the process of the justification of the sinner. St. Thomas had a much more balanced view because he kept more of the traditional *ecclesial* element in the sacrament of penance. "There can be no true contrition without the intention to confess."[27] In other words, St. Thomas was trying to express the fundamental notion that the interior sorrow of the sinner must always be united with the virtue of the passion of Christ; this comes to the sinner only by and through his submission to the Church and her ecclesial penance. Without this will, there can be no true contrition, no forgiveness of sin. Perfect contrition is the point of departure for the sacramental reality and is directed by its very nature to consecration by the Church.[28] Scotus' distinction destroyed this unity and helped to pave the way for the Nominalists of later centuries who further divorced the notion of forgiveness of sin from the Church. This charge is serious enough to warrant a more detailed explanation.

----

[27] St. Thomas, *Comm. in IV Sent.*, D. 17, 2. 5. 2 ad. 1; 3. 1. 4; 3. 5. 1; Quodl. IV, 10; *De Forma Absolutionis*, 6; *In Matth.* 16, 2; *In Joann.* 11, 6, 6.

[28] P. Charles, "Doctrine et pastorale du sacrément de pénitence," in *Nou. Rev. Theo.*, 75 (January, 1953), pp. 449–453; H. Schillebeeckx, *De Sacramentele heilseconomie* (Antwerp, 1952), pp. 355–365.

Synthesis of St. Thomas[29]

The doctrine of St. Thomas starts with his views on the justification of the sinner in general. He says that there are two aspects involved in man's justification: the part of God and the part of man. There can be no justification without a union of these two essential elements: "No sin can be remitted except by means of the passion of Christ. Whence the work of the human will does not suffice for the remission of sin unless there is faith in the passion of Christ and the intention of participating in it by the reception of baptism or submitting oneself to the Keys of the Church."[30] St. Thomas insists on the role of man in the work of salvation (he keeps on repeating the formula of St. Augustine: "God created you without your help, but He will not save you without your help"), or, in his own words, the virtue of penance. But he goes on to say that this virtue of penance has efficacy only because it participates in the passion of Christ through the sacrament of penance confided *only to the Church* (keys of the Church). In other words, if there were no redemptive work of Christ, there would be no remission of sins. Hence, the virtue of penance on the part of man is not sufficient for the remission of sins.

We may conclude, then, that St. Thomas considers penance as a virtue (on the part of man) and as a sacrament (the passion of Christ). Complete penance is a human act but it is also the satisfaction for sin accepted by God through the merits of Jesus Christ. It is only in the union of these two elements that penance is efficacious; therefore in penance there is something active, and this is the human act of sorrow which can be considered the matter (*quasi materia*) of the sacrament. But

---

[29] For abundant bibliography here see the small work of H. Dondaine, *L'attrition suffisante* (Paris, 1943), pp. 18–53 to which we are heavily indebted for this whole section.

[30] *Summa Theologiae*, III, q. 69, a. 1, ad 2; see also *Summa Contra Gentes*, lib. IV, Ch. 72.

there is also something passive which is received gratuitously
by man from God: the sacramental absolution which is nothing
else than the application of the passion of Christ to the sinner
and can be considered the form of penance (quasi forma). The
sacrament of penance is the combination of these two elements.
In order for the virtue of penance to be efficacious it must be
united with the passion of Christ. The union is realized in the
sacrament of penance by the absolution of the priest. This whole
discipline (and notice how St. Thomas keeps the essential
ecclesial character of penance) has been entrusted to the Church
and to her alone.

St. Thomas, therefore, insists on contrition as did Abelard and
the twelfth-century theologians before him. But St. Thomas considered contrition as both an act of the penitent and as a part
of the sacrament. St. Thomas never made the mistake of separat-
ing the two, as did Scotus. Contrition for St. Thomas was sorrow
for sins informed by charity and grace. Attrition was sorrow for
sins, but a sorrow not informed by charity and grace.[31] Above
all, for St. Thomas contrition always included the intention of
receiving the sacrament (hence, submission to ecclesial penance
and unseparable from it). There can be no contrition without
the reception of the sacrament of penance or the will to receive
it (votum Sacramenti).[32] Without going any further into the
Thomistic notion of contrition, it can be concluded that the

---

[31] In IV Sent., D. 16, q. 2. 2. 2: "Talis antem displicentia dolor contritionis dicitur quando est gratia informata." Also De Veritate, 28, 8 and
Contra Gentiles, IV, Ch. 72: "In ipso motu contritionis justificatur poeni-
tens. . . . Tunc autem aliquis justificatur quando gratiam recipit, unde simul
cum gratiae infusione et justificatione est motus contritionis; sed motus at-
tritionis praecedit quasi praeparatorius."

[32] This is the usual way of explaining how a perfect act of contrition
can remit sin outside of the actual reception of the sacrament of penance:
Contrition, then, is the beginning of the sacramental reality of ecclesial
penance and its efficacy is founded on its essential relationship to the sacrament of penance. The Council of Trent seems to have taught this in the
14th session, Ch. 4 (D.B. 898): "Docet praeterea (Synodus) etsi contri-
tionem hanc aliquando caritate perfectam esse contingat hominemque
reconciliare, priusquam sacramentum actu suscipiatur ipsam reconciliationem
ipsi contritioni sine sacramenti voto, quod in illa includitur, non esse
adscribendam. . . ."

great merit of St. Thomas was to have integrated the various elements in the sacrament of penance. Confession is therefore necessary because it is included in contrition; it is a necessary element of contrition. There is, then, a perfect integration of the part of the penitent in the sacrament of penance. The personal element, the divine element, and the ecclesial element are all coordinated and joined in the doctrine of St. Thomas.

The Synthesis of Duns Scotus[33]

Like St. Thomas, Duns Scotus starts his doctrine from the notion of the justification of the sinful man. Scotus distinguishes two elements in every mortal sin. First, he notes habitual individual injustice by which sinful man is deprived of sanctifying grace. It is called a habit because the sinner in mortal sin remains in a state devoid of sanctifying grace. In other words, the privation of this grace remains even after the act of sin has passed. Second, Scotus teaches that the sinful man has an obligation to undergo the penalty due because of the sin (the guilt of sin). This obligation is present in the very essence of a man's soul because of the sin he has committed.

But how is the justification of the sinful man brought about? It is here that Scotus disagrees with St. Thomas. First of all, the habitual injustice of the sinner must be destroyed. This is done by the infusion of sanctifying grace through the merits of Jesus Christ. From this doctrine, a very dangerous conclusion can be drawn (a conclusion that is logically developed by the Nominalists). If the infusion of grace is done through the merits of Jesus Christ, God can infuse grace without any free cooperation on the part of man, even if man is able to cooperate. St. Thomas, on the other hand, integrated the part of man and the merits of Christ perfectly in the one sacrament of penance which exists in the Church.

Scotus developed a twofold idea on penance (and this is

---

33 H. Dondaine, *op. cit.*, pp. 40–46.

where he profoundly differs from St. Thomas). Because God's mercy is so great, He has given man two types (*viae*) of penance.[34] The "first way" is that of sufficient attrition. This is a justification which comes from man's good intention, a movement of the soul which disposes man to receive grace *de congruo*. Hence, Scotus explains, there are different stages in sorrow for sin, for a man's sorrow can increase. Then, when God judges that this sorrow is sufficient, He infuses grace into the soul of the sinner (*attritus fit contritus*).[35] According to Scotus, God has willed that attrition should last for a certain time. When it has lasted long enough it becomes sufficient to merit *de congruo* justification and God's grace. By that very fact, then, the sinner's attrition becomes contrition.[36] The normal conclusion of this type of reasoning is that, since the sinner has sufficient attrition, it is not necessary that the sinner receive the sacrament of penance. Scotus saves his orthodoxy, however, by saying that all mortal sins must be expressed in the sacrament of penance because God willed that this be done through His instituted sacrament. But even in this case, the sacrament does not remit sin; it only increases sanctifying grace.

The "second way" to expiate sin is through the sacrament of penance. This is principally for those who do not have sufficient attrition to merit the remission of their sins *de congruo*. There are two conditions for its valid and fruitful reception: the person must will to receive the sacrament and he must not put an obstacle (*non ponere obicem*) in the way of the infusion of grace; that is, his will must not remain attached to the sin committed. The sinner must be well disposed by having a cer-

---

[34] Scotus arrived at this notion by means of comparison with the adult who is to be baptized. The adult can gain grace either by the good disposition of his free will (*ex merito de congruo*) or by actual baptism in which he receives grace by the promise of God (*ex pacto divino*).

[35] This expression is obscure. For its origins see P. Anciaux, "Le sens de l'adage *Ex attrito fit contritus* Chez Pierre Lombard, S. Albert le Grand, Guillaume d'Auvergne et S. Thomas d'Aquin," an offprint doctrinal dissertation (Louvain, 1947).

[36] Duns Scotus defines contrition in the same way as St. Thomas, cf. n. 31.

tain aversion for sin. In this context, the sacrament of penance is necessary of itself since the sins cannot be remitted by way of sufficient attrition. Here the sinner is justified by God and not by his own merits. But even here Scotus maintains that the essential of the sacrament of penance lies in the absolution of the priest. The acts of the penitent are not essential parts of the sacrament, but only the preambles or conditions of the sacrament. They are what is termed as integral parts (*partes integrantes*), that is, that for the sacrament to be complete as God willed it, these acts should be present. For Scotus, then, the sacrament of penance does not have any matter properly so called, only a form. The whole strength of the sacrament lies in the absolution.

Scotus cannot be accused of laxism. He does not say that sins can be forgiven no matter how the sinner receives the sacrament. He considers the part of the penitent as a true preamble which necessarily includes a certain aversion (*displicentia*) to sin. Yet, the separation inherent in the "two ways" is extremely dangerous. The balance of the personal, ecclesial, and divine elements which were well developed in St. Thomas are here endangered. Scotus saved orthodoxy by requiring a submission to the sacrament of penance even in his famous "first way" (sufficient attrition) by virtue of the divine will. Later Nominalists make the complete break between the penitent's contrition and the sacrament of penance. In the words of the famous scholar of penance, H. Dondaine: "Duns Scotus distinguishes two parallel types of justification, repentance and the sacrament. . . . The separation begun with Scotus is complete with the Nominalists."[37]

The charge against Scotus of forgetting the basic ecclesial character of sacramental penance is justified. What St. Thomas united under the authority of the keys in one union of the merits of Christ applied to the sorrow of the penitent is shifted from the Church to the direct relationship between God and

37 H. Dondaine, *op. cit.*, p. 46.

the sinner. The relationship established by Scotus of the sacrament of penance with the Church, which is simply the divine will, is precarious. In the Nominalists we have the complete break and consequently the complete destruction of the ecclesial mark of penance; the stage is thus set for the violent controversies between contritionalists and attritionalists.

CONCLUSION

Reconciliation with the Church is today considered by most theologians as the *res et sacramentum* of the sacrament of penance. This modern advancement in theological thought is due to a more penetrating historical analysis of the first ten centuries of the Church; ignorance of this period was, in no small measure, responsible for this neglect in the scholastic period. In spite of this handicap, St. Thomas admirably constructed a well-integrated doctrine of penance, simultaneously respecting the personal, divine, and ecclesial aspects of the one sacrament of penance. Duns Scotus continued the more familiar scholastic tradition of separation in the diverse elements of the sacrament of penance, and this only led to a further confusion in later centuries. Modern research on the history of penance combined with the doctrine of St. Thomas has brought a greater understanding of the essential role of the Church in penance.

CHAPTER VIII

The Existence of Penance as a Sacrament in the Church

INTRODUCTION

The brief history of penance in the early Church has served to show that penance is a providential remedy for sin in the Church. The full reconciliation of the sinner with God is accomplished only in the submission of the sinner to ecclesial penance and by reconciliation with the Church. Outside the Church, then, there can be no forgiveness of sin, no friendship with God after grievous sin. The self-accusation (confession) of the sinner and his detestation of sin had to be brought to him who held the power of the keys in the Church, the bishop. Under his authority and direction, the sinner was excommunicated from the Eucharistic banquet and made to perform public penance for his sins. This done, the penitent again returned to the Church and to her essential minister, the bishop, to be reconciled with the Church and by that action with God Himself. "The reconciliation with the altar" was now complete. "By the intervention of the Church, the expiation of the sinner was brought to bear in a visible and efficacious fashion on the passion of Christ to bring about the destruction of sin and establishing the living union with God."[1]

There remain, however, two very serious problems to be examined in the next two chapters. The first is whether this practice of penance in the Church can be called a true sacrament. In other words, does the visibility of this practice of penance, as examined, constitute an efficacious sign of God's forgiveness and saving power? On what human and divine elements will this depend? What principles from man's own nature and from the

[1] P. Anciaux, Le Sacrément de la Pénitence (Louvain, 1960), p. 96.

divine economy can be invoked to justify the efficacious visibility of the sacrament of penance? This will be the subject matter of the present chapter. The sacramentality of penance depends on the efficaciousness of the mysteries of Christ, by whose life, death, and resurrection all men have been saved. Yet these mysteries reach man only through the visible acts of the Church where his salvation is effectively accomplished in Christ. In other words, God saves man according to his nature through the visibility of Christ's body, the visibility of the Church, and finally, the visibility of man's own nature. For as the visibility of man belongs to the essence of his nature, or, as St. Thomas says: "The soul is united to the body for the sake of the act of understanding, which is its proper and principal act: wherefore the body that is united to the soul has to be perfectly adapted to serve the soul in everything required for its act of thought";[2] so too, in the divine plan, the body of Christ was essential in the mystery of man's redemption.[3] By the Incarnation, the human body and its visibility found the capacity for expression carried to the infinite, for now it expresses God. The face of Christ was literally the human face of God. The continuation of this visible manifestation of the mercy of God in Christ is continued in the visible Church, which is Christ "communicated and spread abroad." For as Pius XII so beautifully expresses it, the Church in her visible structure is nothing more than the continuation of the visibility of the humanity of Christ.[4]

---

[2] St. Thomas, *De Anima*, art. VIII, 15.

[3] L. Cerfaux, *Christ in the Theology of St. Paul* (New York, 1959), p. 166; see also the excellent work on this subject by J. Mouroux, *The Meaning of Man* (New York, 1948), pp. 80–81. It remains true, however, that there are two theories on salvation — that of St. John and that of St. Paul (that is, salvation through the Incarnation [St. John] and through the Resurrection [St. Paul]). Essentially, they do not contradict each other, but they do begin from two different points of view; one from the death and resurrection of Christ, the other from the totality of the mystery of salvation in the Incarnation itself; see the penetrating study of P. Daubercies, *La Condition Charnelle* (Tournai, 1958), pp. 15–72.

[4] Pius XII, encyclical letter, *Mystici Corporis Christi*, Chap. 15 (Paulist ed.); also J. A. Jungmann, "L'Eglise dans la Vie Religieuse d'Aujourdhui," *L'Eglise est Une; Hommage à Moehler*, ed. P. Chaillet, pp. 333–348.

These three elements are wonderfully projected in the sacramentality of God's salvific plan for men. His logic, so to speak, was perfect in dealing with men. The visibility of the sacraments themselves is but a further extension of this principle. An attempt will be made to justify each of these three elements in applying them more particularly to the sacrament of penance. This will be the matter of the present chapter.

I. SACRAMENTALITY OF MAN

This chapter begins with an anthropology, or a study of man in his concrete reality. Modern philosophers and psychologists have demonstrated the aspect of man's incarnation or involvement in matter. This aspect of his nature is not something accidental or secondary but pertains to the very order of his being. Man's body is part and parcel of his very existence, and without it he would cease to be a man. In the words of St. Thomas, man is a combination or better yet an intimate union of spirit and matter: *ratio et manus*. He is then an incarnate spirit who functions and lives his relationships in the world. Even in the most spiritual acts, the body is still needed. The hand of the artist and the hand of the surgeon are at the service of their minds, but the latter incarnate themselves only in and through matter.[5] The operation which saves can only produce its effect in and through matter, the surgeon's experienced hands working to save. The soul, then, has an absolute need of the body to incarnate its thought and intelligence into the objective world of values. But what exactly is the relationship between this corporeality and the spirit which animates this corporeality?

The first observation of this phenomenological[6] study is the

---

[5] For a summary of the diverse elements of this chapter, see A. Dondeyne, *Contemporary European Thought and Christian Faith* (Pittsburgh, 1958), pp. 36–66.

[6] We use this term in the present context in the sense of Pierre Teilhard de Chardin, namely, only an observation of man or a description of man's external reality. Cf. *The Phenomenon of Man* (New York, 1959), p. 35. Thus our approach will be the concrete order of being such as it is re-

basic fact that the body is part and parcel of the universe, of the material world. This observation is so evident and so strong that whole philosophies have been constructed on this element of man's reality. To use a more modern approach, what is not directly verifiable in the experience of the positive sciences is taken to be uncertain; a further step concludes that all other reality does not exist or can be reduced to natural and material phenomena.[7] This is a spontaneous tendency of the mind and it unceasingly threatens thinking and spoils even the best efforts to describe man and his place in the universe. It is impossible to refute this sort of a philosophy in any *a priori* fashion; what must be shown, however, is that this materialism is based on an incomplete description of man taken in the totality of the phenomena of his concrete existence.

In any case, the body remains part of the material universe. It is controlled to a very great degree by the spatio-temporal laws which govern every material object. In this sense, then, the individual is placed into a situation he cannot change. A man is not completely free to do as he pleases in the physical and material world of reality. It is, in the words of P. Ricoeur, a "consent to reality" which the individual cannot change.[8] A man must consent to these physical laws which rule him and which have objectively been given to him at birth; his physical makeup, his temperament, his character, to a very large degree, can never be totally changed. A man has been partly determined by heredity and the rest of his historical past. This sense of historical past is so strong that many modern psychologists, as well as philosophers, have proposed that man is determined by these given elements. This sense of historicity or becoming is perhaps the most characteristic trait of recent times. Whatever the errors in this domain, the merit of this description is that man sees

---

vealed to us and presents us with a definite sense, a sense which makes us experience our existence in relationship with ourselves, others, and the external world.

[7] Dondeyne, *op. cit.*, pp. 13–15.

[8] *La Philosophie de la Volunté*, I (Paris, 1952), p. 38; Hans Reiner, *Freiheit, Wollen und Aktivität*, pp. 68–73.

more clearly than ever before that his freedom and liberty are not absolute. In many respects never dreamed of by the ancients, man is limited by the very constitution of his nature.

There is, however, another essential element in man, his spirit. Although man is part of the material universe, he has a subjectivity whereby he views himself to be the very source of his actions and activities. It is an "operation which does not pass into any external reality but remains in the subject as its perfection."[9] He knows himself to be the subject of his free acts whereby he acts upon the surrounding world. The body, however, which is an essential part of a man's being, serves to limit these free acts in the sense described above. The consequence is that man is neither pure matter nor pure spirit and, in this sense, it is the totality of man which operates, thinks, works, etc. "The soul is neither all of me nor is my body."[10] In actions, it is the total composite which acts and with the result that, for man, there can be no purely spiritual act. This is nothing more than the consequence of man's substantial union of body and soul. Moderns are correct in applying to man the term of "incarnate spirit," for every action of man receives the imprint both of his body and his soul. To separate them, to emphasize one at the cost of the other is to be unfaithful to the simple description of man's actions. Philosophically, it is to fall into the opposite errors of naturalism (materialism) or intellectualism (idealism), both of which fail to take the totality of the description into consideration.[11]

The body is fundamental to man's being and it intervenes in each of his actions. It forms part of the subject which he is. Yet, by the spirit, he is unlimited in his capacity. Man is not a closed being, an interiority, which exists in and for itself. Insofar as a man is spiritual he is open to reality, all reality. The spirit,

---

[9] St. Thomas, *De Veritate*, q. 7, art. 6, *in Corpore*.

[10] St. Thomas, *Super Epistolas S. Pauli Lectura*, I (Super Primam Epistolam ad Corinthios, Caput II, Lectio I).

[11] Dondeyne, *op. cit.*, p. 3; see also the article of A. De Waelhens, "Phenomenologie et Metaphysique," in *Revue Phil. de Louvain*, 47 (1949), pp. 365–374.

in the words of St. Thomas following Aristotle, is, in a sense, all things.[12] It is through this very possibility as an incarnate spirit that man can change the world from a physical reality to a cultural reality by giving meaning and signification to the physical world. In a very true sense, the definition of work is the fruit of the spirit. And since work is man's most fundamental activity it is easy to see that work is the product of the incarnate spirit which is man. The dialectic between man and nature is in the very essence of man. Man is neither pure spirit nor pure matter, but an incarnate spirit. That is why man perfects himself by perfecting the world around him; he humanizes himself to the degree that he humanizes the world around him by his work and activity. "Man is essentially *artifex*, creator of forms and art. . . ."[13] Certain types of work demand more or less a participation of the spirit than the body and vice versa, but all types demand a participation of both under pain of ceasing to be human.[14]

This analysis of man has permitted a verification that none of man's actions are purely spiritual. In other words, God has created man as incarnate spirit and what is discovered in this description of man is nothing more than the intention of the Creator manifesting itself in man's incarnate nature.[15] The totality of what a man is intervenes in each of his actions. The knowledge he has of even spiritual realities comes from an analogy with the material universe with which he is acquainted, e.g., the soul, a breath; angel, ambassador; etc. In each of these cases symbols are employed and without these symbols man would understand nothing of God. Even thought must be clothed in material symbols. St. Thomas understood this very well when he said that the knowledge of spiritual realities is attained only

---

[12] "Unaquaeque intellectualis substantia est quodam modo omnia, in quantum totius entis comprehensiva est suo intellectu," *Contra Gentes*, III, 112.

[13] M. D. Chenu, *Pour Une Théologie du Travail* (Paris, 1955), p. 17; *Foi et Technique* (XIII Assemblee Pleniere de Pax Romana), p. 20.

[14] *Foi et Technique* (Paris, 1960), p. 22.

[15] L. Janssens, *Droits Personnels et Autorité* (Louvain, 1954), p. 17.

by "comparisons, negations, and the way of excellence." Man has no direct intuition of spiritual realities.

Even more important than man's relations and communication with the object world is his relationship with others. It becomes very clear that this is simply impossible without the intervention of the body which expresses and communicates the feelings of the soul. In the world of human reality, individuals live their relationships with others, person to person in an "I-thou" relationship. There is a basic dialectic between man and the physical reality around him; but only in the interpersonal relationship of "I-thou" can he have reciprocity and dialogue in the true sense of the word. The dialogue reveals that the other is a person, an *alter ego*, who is also free, who thinks, wills, suffers, loves, etc. It reveals that the other is no longer an object as are the material things of the physical world to be "worked upon"; the other is a subject, a person who is similar to ourselves.

But even here, corporeality is fundamental and inescapable in developing interpersonal relationships. Bodies act as a sign which can either reveal or hide what is in the soul. The body is the possibility of approach in the relationship of respect, fidelity, etc., with others. When a boy loves a girl, he must communicate that love by signs, a kiss, an embrace, etc. The first sign is the body and all others are but extensions of this one fundamental sign. The order of love directly intends the person but it can only attain the beloved by means of a sign which is expressed by and through the body. "The soul forms and trains its body in order to seize itself: the body's activity enables the soul to express itself to itself and achieve self-awareness."[16] A man and woman incarnate their love in a child; a painter in his painting; a technician in his art, and so forth throughout the whole gamut of human reality. There can be no

---

[16] J. Mouroux, *op. cit.*, p. 46; H. Lhermitte, *L'Image de Notre Corps* (Paris, 1956), pp. 156–157. See interesting study on this universality of the Kingdom of Christ in J. Leclercq, *l'Idée de la Royauté du Christ au Moyen Age* (Paris, 1959).

full love without expression; there can be no expression without the intermediary of the body.

The conclusion of this phenomenological description is quite simple: a man cannot arrive at any human or spiritual reality without the intermediary of corporeality. It is the totality of man as an incarnate spirit which must be taken into consideration in every action he does. From an examination of these objective data it can be seen that God has created us in this way, as incarnate spirits. We will see that when God intervenes by supernatural means into the life of man, He must respect what He Himself has created under pain of destroying what He created. He must consider the needs of man's nature if He wants our cooperation in communicating grace which works by signs incarnated in external things. The old scholastic adage could not be truer: "God does not destroy nature but presupposes and builds on it."

II. THE SACRAMENTALITY OF CHRIST

"And the Word was made flesh and dwelt among us; and we saw his glory . . ." In these few words, the beloved disciple describes the essential core of salvation. The essential theme of the theology of St. John was that the Son of God became a man and that man could gaze on God through Christ. The veils of His humanity were to reveal God's "glory," which is the Hebrew word for the very being of God. The visibility of the Incarnate Word played a major role in the theology of the fourth evangelist. It is the sacramentality of the Son of God: the Son reveals Himself as He is by visible signs which permit men to see what is hidden behind those signs and veils — the Divine Word Himself. God could not reveal Himself to men as He was. Men were neither capable of it nor did it become God to bring man to Himself without man's faith in Him. God, therefore, chose the perfect instrument in the sacramentality and visibility of the humanity of His Son. In signs, as John calls all of Christ's miracles, the Word Incarnate reveals Himself to men. These signs are but signs, that is, they make an appeal to men's faith. They are sufficient to draw men if they will humbly accept God's way. But being visible signs, they do not compel men to faith in the Son of God.[17] The theme of the miracle, the sign in St. John's Gospel, is that it permits men to contemplate the divinity of Christ but does not compel them. Miracles are a divine appeal to men's faith in Christ as the only-begotten Son.

The Incarnation, then, is the visible manifestation of the Word to men. The Word was from all eternity with God and became man to dwell among us (Jn 1:14). In his Incarnate Person, then, God has become visible to men and knowable by them. "On God no man ever laid his eyes; the only begotten Son who rests in the Father's bosom, has himself been the interpreter" (Jn 1:18). God's love prompted Him to send His own Son — the *agapé* — which was stressed so often by the Synoptic Gospels in the parables of the Good Samaritan, the Good Shepherd, the Prodigal Son, etc.[18] This love was communicated and manifested visibly to men by the coming of the only-begotten Son as a victim for men's sins (Jn 4:13). Thus men are given the unique way of knowing something about God, of arriving at salvation by the visible incarnation of the Son of God. Men cannot know God in an immediate fashion on earth, but the Father is revealed in His incarnate and visible Son. To see Jesus is to see the Father. We cannot bypass Christ, the visible Christ, to attain the invisible God directly. There is no frustration in this mode of thought, for Christ is the perfect image of the Father. That is why the Fourth Gospel insists on the fundamental duty of faith to see the Father as visibly manifested in the Incarnate Son. "The invisible God has become visible; the

---

[17] For a complete study of the sign-parabolic theme in the Gospel of St. John, see the magnificent study of L. Cerfaux, "Les Miracles, Signes Messianiques de Jésus et Oeuvres de Dieu Selon l'Evangile de Saint Jean," in *Recueil Lucien Cerfaux*, II, pp. 41–50.

[18] Mt 9:36; 14:14; Lk 7:13; 15:30. See J. Danielou, "Le Bon Samaritain," in *Melanges Bibliques Religiés en l'Honneur de A. Robert* (Paris, 1958), pp. 456–465.

Son of God has descended from heaven in a human nature in order to reveal Him and by thus introducing us into the divine filiation, has introduced us into His knowledge and love."[19]

Thus the love of God is made known to us in Christ. This love is a totally free gift of Himself to men. It is God who takes the initiative and establishes the communion of His love with men. As a matter of fact, St. John defines God as love.[20] This theology is summed up in the First Epistle of St. John. "God's love was made manifest among us by the fact that God sent his only-begotten Son into the world that we might have life through him. This love consists not in our having loved God but in his having loved us and his having sent his Son as a propitiation for our sins" (1 Jn 4:9–10). This love of God is communicated to us by the visible incarnation of the Son of God both positively (the giving of the divine life) and negatively (the remission of our sins).

St. Paul also insisted on the love of God which has been communicated to us by the incarnation of Christ. Yet Paul insists more on the death and the resurrection of Christ as a proof of God's love for men. "While we were still helpless, Christ . . . died for us wicked people. Why, it is only with difficulty that a person will die to save a good man. Yes, it is only for a worthy person that a man may, perhaps, have the courage to face death. But God proves his love for us, because, when we were still sinners, Christ died for us. . . . Surely, if when we were enemies we were reconciled to God by the death of his Son; much more, once we are reconciled, shall we be saved by his life" (Rom 5:6–10). The meaning of the passage is clear. St. Paul tells us that a giving love is difficult and that the greatness of the love of God appears in the fact that God loved us when we were His enemies since we were sinners. As a consequence, argues

---

[19] Francois Amiot, "Deum Nemo Unquam Vidit," in *Melanges Bibliques Religiés en l'Honneur de A. Robert*, pp. 470–477. See also D. Mollat, "Le Semeion Johannique," in *Sacra Pagina*, II, 209–218; R. Schnackenburg, "Die Sakramente im Johannes Evangelium," in *Sacra Pagina*, II, pp. 235–254.

[20] The definitive study on *agapé* in the N. T. by C. Spicq, *Agapé dans le Nouveau Testament*, 3V. (Paris, 1958–1961).

St. Paul, the death of Christ on the cross is a clear manifestation of God's love for men. Thus God communicates Himself through the blood of Christ and His death on the cross.[21] "The charity of Christ is the revelation of God's charity. Christ gives Himself up, and God gives Him up for us. 'He . . . has not spared his own Son but has delivered him for us all' " (Rom 8:32).[22]

In summary, the objective redemption is accomplished for men because of God's love for them. For St. John and St. Paul, more concretely, the Incarnation, the Passion, and all the mysteries of the body of Christ are the indispensable means of the communication of God's love to men. God has saved men through the visible instrumentality of His only-begotten Son. This then is the primary sacrament in the Christian economy of salvation: the humanity of Christ. This humanity is the sacrament joined to the divinity which has brought about salvation. Christ's humanity is above all the primary sacrament *because it is the sign which manifested and communicated the very love of God*. Father Y. Congar has explained this very well when commenting on the teaching of St. Thomas in this matter: "Christ, in His humanity joined to the divinity *in persona*, has a true and particular causality, though instrumental. St. Thomas revives a teaching of the Greek Fathers, especially St. Cyril of Alexandria and St. John Damascene, when he calls Christ the organ, the conjoined instrument, having its causality in the giving; a living instrument, having its initiative, while entering the situation by human knowledge and human will. . . . Moreover, Christ in His glorious humanity, humanizes the divine life communicated. . . . Christ has become a member and individual

---

[21] It was the favorite phrase of all the Fathers of the Church to say: "*qui propter immensam suam dilectionem factus est quod sumus nos, uti nos perficeret esse quod est ipse*," St. Irenaeus, *Adversus Haer.*, V. proem; St. Athanasius, *De Incarnatione*, 56 (P.G., 25, c. 192B). "Having been born of a woman according to the flesh, He took to Himself the body He had taken from her, in order to take root among us by means of an indissoluble union and to make us stronger than death and corruption," St. Cyril of Alexandria, *In Lukam*, V, 19 (P.G., 72, c. 192B).

[22] L. Cerfaux, *Christ in the Theology of St. Paul* (New York, 1959), p. 125.

among the general concourse of humanity and therefore He can
rise to be its head so that it becomes His body."[23]

III. THE SACRAMENTALITY OF THE CHURCH

All of Christ's sanctifying power has now passed to the Church.
The relationship between Christ and the Church is the all-
important link in the economy of salvation. For just as God
willed to take on a visible human nature in order to teach and
lead men as they were, so too this very element of sacramentality,
the visibility of Christ's saving powers, becomes the very basis
of His Church. What then is this relationship between Christ
and the Church?[24]

What does an examination of the doctrine of Scripture in regard to this relationship reveal? St. Paul's doctrine is complex
but can be approached from a detailed analysis of the evolution of his thought in the greater Epistles and those of the
captivity.[25] In the Epistle to the Colossians, St. Paul says of
Christ: "For in him is embodied and dwells the fullness of the
Godhead" (plerôma somatikos) (Col 2:9). This is the same
theme previously examined above in which the love of God and
all His gifts are present in Christ the man, and that in a corporeal
way by His humanity. The history of the word plerôma is extremely complicated, and no attempt at exegesis is made here.
Suffice it to say that the word in this context means that in
Christ the divinity lives in a corporeal way, above all in the
body that He took from His Mother. The text also means that
the Godhead dwells in all of humanity insofar as Christ is their
source of grace and union with God. Above all in the resur-

---

[23] Y. Congar, The Mystery of the Church (Baltimore, 1959), p. 109; see
St. Thomas, Summa Theologiae, III, q. 62, a. 5.

[24] For valuable insights into this present question see the important work
of Otto Semmelroth, Die Kirche als Ursakrament (Frankfurt am Main,
1953), espec. pp. 61–124. Also valuable study by E. H. Schillebeeckx,
"The Sacraments: An Encounter with God," in Christianity Divided (New
York, 1961), pp. 245–278.

[25] This, of course, is the thesis of Msgr. L. Cerfaux in his magnificent
book, The Church in the Theology of St. Paul (New York, 1959), pp. 7–8.

rected body of Christ is constituted, through the Holy Spirit, the principle of new life and sanctification for all men. By communication with Christ, men participate in this divine life given by the Incarnate Word.[26] In another revealing text, placing the resurrected body with the body of the Church, St. Paul says: "And [he] has appointed him [Christ] sovereign head of the Church, which is truly his body, the complement of him who fills all the members with all graces" (Eph 1:22-23). Here we have a direct relation between the fullness of sanctifying powers in the resurrected body of Christ and the body of the Church. What is this relationship? Since the plenitude or fullness of the divinity is the body of Christ and the Church is the body of Christ, the plenitude of the divinity resides also in the Church and that in a corporeal way as in Christ. The visible reality must be maintained in both relationships, or the value of the comparison is completely destroyed. The plenitude of Christ's sanctifying powers is now in the world by means of external things, by means of sacramental signs which are the Church (the *sacramentum separatum*, in the words of the scholastics). In the words of Monsignor Cerfaux: "And so we can say that Christ is the sanctifying fulness of Christians. In keeping with this formula, but taking *plerôma* in the passive and concrete sense to mean the entirety of those who receive life and sanctification from Christ, Paul writes that the Church is the body of Christ, His *plerôma*, that is to say, the sphere in which is exercised the power of life and sanctification of him who 'fills' holiness completely in all. . . . The Church is thus the sphere in which the divine life which passes through Christ, finds its full flavor."[27] The two bodies (of Christ and the Church) are mystically identified. The glorious visible body of Christ is the inhabitation of the *plerôma*; by identification with this body, the Church receives the whole of this sanctifying power (*plerôma*). Just as the glori-

---

[26] For a full history of this word and its use in the epistles of the Captivity see P. Benoit, "Corps, Tête et Plérôme dans les Epîtres de la Captivité," in *Revue Biblique*, 60 (1956), pp. 5–44.

[27] L. Cerfaux, *op. cit.*, pp. 323–325.

ous body of Christ is the outflowing of His Person and therefore of all sanctifying power, this is also true of the visible Church which has become mystically identified with the glorious body of Christ. In reality, there are not two bodies but one.[28]

This union between Christ and the Church is the foundation of the whole sacramental system in the visibility of its communication. Since the body of Christ is the preeminent sacrament in the sense explained above,[29] in almost the same way the Church, as His body, communicates the divine life. With regard to all the seven sacraments, the Church can be rightly called the fundamental sacrament, because by these seven sacred signs, the Church communicates this divine life. "The seven sacraments are the actualization of the potentials of the fundamental sacrament which is the Church."[30]

This was a fundamental tradition among all the Fathers of the Church. To quote but one of the greatest witnesses, "The historical facts of the life of Christ have a divine power and this power of the mysteries of Christ live on in the efficacy of the Sacraments."[31] In the sacraments, the power of Christ reaches us, explains St. Augustine, and these sacraments are in the Church. That is why the ancient Fathers insisted on the fact that outside the Church there can be no salvation. How nonbelievers were saved was another problem for them; what was absolutely certain was that, in some way, this salvation had to come through the visible Church, for this was and is an essential element in her basic constitution.

In this same vein the great modern theologian, M. J. Scheeben, was able to say: "The causality of the sacraments is to be found

---

[28] J. Huby, Epîtres de la Captivité (Verbum Salutis), p. 169.

[29] See how the Council of Trent defines a sacrament: "symbolum rei sacrae et invisibilis gratiae forma visibilis" (D.B. 876). In this sense, then, our description of the humanity of Christ and of the Church is eminently correct.

[30] "Die Einzelnen Sakramente (sind) die Aktualisierung des Potentiellen Ursakramentes Kirche, das Sich in Sie Hinein und Durch Sie in die Einzelheiten des Menschlichen Lebens Ausgliert," c. Semmelroth, op. cit., p. 57.

[31] St. Augustine, Enchiridion Theologicum Sancti Augustini (BAC, N. 205), pp. 620–621.

not so much in a paradoxical efficacy, in the supernatural order, of a rite of perceptible action, as in the existence of a society, which under the appearances of a human institution hides a divine reality."[32] This same theologian, then, insists on calling all the sacraments the sacraments of the Church, which they really are.

By this union with Christ the Church herself is sacramental. In this mystical union which we have described, the powers of Christ are transferred to the visible Church. All the powers of Christ — of order, of teaching, and of jurisdiction — are transferred now to the Church, which must carry out the work of salvation which Christ has bequeathed to it. Thus, God has respected here the same order of redemption as He had done in the order of the creation of man: the sacramentality and visibility of the saving powers of Christ's humanity have been forever transferred to the humanity and visibility of the Church. *Homo, Christus Jesus* — mediation of the man-Christ, for men; all in this is homogeneous with man, connatural with him; that is to say, that it is both sensible and spiritual, personal and collective, interior and exterior. The sacraments, like the Church as a whole, are a prolongation of the incarnation of the Word and follow out, in their scheme and manner, the logic of its theandric character.[33]

IV. Application to the Sacrament of Penance

How does the sacrament of penance fit into the scheme of God's economy of salvation? Our short study of the history of penance has served to show how perfectly penance fits into this divine economy of salvation. The whole apparatus of public penance and pardon made it clear that the reconciliation of the

---

[32] *The Mysteries of Christianity* (St. Louis, 1954), pp. 558–566.

[33] Y. Congar, *op. cit.*, p. 130; see as well St. Tromp, "De Biformi Conceptu cum Christi Mystici tum Corporis Christi in Controversiis S. R. Bellarmini," in *Gregorianum*, 23 (1942), 279–290; E. Elorduy, "El Cuerpo Mistico de Cristo en Suarez," in *Rev. Españ., de Téol.*, 3 (1943), 347–397.

sinner is in the first place a reconciliation with the Church; this constitutes an efficacious sign of reconciliation with God.[34]

In the primitive discipline of penance there is a clear and visible intervention by the Church in the form of her qualified ministers, the bishops and the priests. This is most clear in examining any of the texts from the earliest times in the Church (*supra*, pp. 79–90). The visible reconciliation is twofold. In the first place by the prayer and help given the public penitents. (In the words of St. Augustine: "When the Church prays, Christ prays.") All the faithful were assembled each Sunday to pray with the bishop and the presbyters. There the whole community prayed for the *ordo poenitentium* in order that they might gain the grace needed to accomplish the penance previously imposed by the bishop. The basic meaning of the word "ecclesial" when used in reference to penance is clear: the faithful were assembled (the *Ecclesia* or assembly of God[35]) to pray as a group for these public sinners. So too, at particular penitential periods during the year, especially during Lent, the community was assembled more frequently to pray for them.[36] Even in private penance this task of praying for the sinner in the name of the whole Church belonged to the priest who received the confession. He was to help the penitent also by his counsel and advice. He acted in a very strict sense in the place of the Church.

In the second place, this visible intervention of the Church is clearly seen in the juridical intervention through the power of the Church. Thus we have the liturgical excommunication im-

---

[34] H. De Lubac, *Catholicism* (London, 1955), p. 37.

[35] "Universi enim quae ex Aegypto profectio fiebat, a Deo typus et imago fuit profectionis Ecclesiae, quae erat futura ex Gentibus," St. Irenaeus, *Adv. Haer.*, IV, 47. See also L. Cerfaux, "La Première Communauté Chrétienne à Jerusalem," in *Eph. Theol. Lov.*, 16 (1939), 22–28; K. L. Schmidt, art. "Ekklesia," in *Theolog. Wörterbuch*, V. III, p. 508.

[36] This aspect of ecclesial prayer is often forgotten today. The *obligation* to pray for sinners is a very serious duty *ex charitate* on the part of all the faithful. Even in the present liturgy, some form of this ancient discipline has been kept as when the priest prays in the place of the whole Church (*Misereatur*, etc., before the absolution of sin).

posed by the bishop, and as the "guardian of the sacraments," he also imposed the penance according to the gravity of the sin and the sincerity of the penitent. Finally, the reconciliation "with the altar" which "remits the eternal pains" that the sins incurred was indeed efficacious, as all the Fathers argued, because, "What you shall loose on earth shall be loosed also in heaven." In private penance, this same phenomenon is present. The confession is received by a qualified minister of the Church. He gives the penance and reconciles the sinner in the name of the Church and in the name of God.

This intervention of the Church in penance makes it a sacrament, for the prayer of the Church is the prayer of Christ. Her prayer, in a strict sense, effects an infallible reconciliation of the sinner with herself and, by that act, with God as it was promised to her by Christ Himself. Certainly, there can be no sacrament just because of the Church's prayer alone, but because this prayer and this juridical intervention are connected with the power given to the Church by Christ (Mt 18:16). "The pastoral power, the authority to impose penance and to accord reconciliation, is here united to the power of order, in virtue of which these acts of the Church have a sanctifying value. The two powers are intimately joined in the minister of penance. . . . Thus, reconciliation with the Church is the *efficacious sign* of the reconciliation with God."[37] The Fathers of the Church kept insisting that outside of the Church there can be no forgiveness of sin. Only by submission to the Church can man have any guarantee of a union with God. Penance is efficacious in virtue of the Church and not vice versa. It is efficacious because it is a visible extension of the Church to the sinner which, in its turn, is nothing more than the extension of the Incarnation of Christ. It is efficacious because it is ecclesial and it is ecclesial because the Church "is truly his body, the complement (*plerôma*) of him who fulfills all members with all graces" (Eph 1:23).

---

[37] P. Anciaux, *op. cit.*, p. 97; see also B. Poschmann, "Die Innere Struktur des Bussakrament," in *Münchner Theologischen Zeitschrift*, 3 (1950), 13–20.

CONCLUSION

It is evident, now, why St. Thomas insists so strongly on submission to the Church.[38] The submission of the sinner to ecclesial penance is the absolute condition for any true contrition. There can be no reconciliation with God without the reconciliation with Church which is performed through the confession and penance of the sinner.

The whole of this process coincides with the divine economy of creation and redemption. Christ appears in the visible form of humanity to show men the way to God in a fashion men can understand, since man is essentially an incarnate spirit. This incarnation is continued on earth through His visible fullness which is the Church. Through an extension of Christ's forgiving mercy given to the Church, the sinner is visibly reconciled to the Church in ecclesial penance which is the infallible *sign* of his reconciliation with God.

---

[38] Among many texts of St. Thomas, see *Commentarium in IV Sent.*, D. 17, 2. 5. 2 ad 1; 3. 1. 4; 3. 5. 1; *Quodlib.*, IV, 10; *In Mattheum* 16, 2; *In Joann.* 11, 6, 6.

CHAPTER IX

The Evolution of the Sacrament of Penance

INTRODUCTION

A final important problem to be considered is that of the theological notion of the sacrament of penance as instituted by Christ.[1] The external structure of the sacrament of penance has evolved radically from that which was used in the early Church. But the inner reality has always remained unchanged: the power to forgive sin in the Church through her qualified ministers, the bishops. How can this sacrament, which was instituted by Christ, change its external structure and still remain fundamentally the same reality established by Christ? A sacrament of the New Law cannot be defined without including its immediate institution by Christ.[2] This would seem to pose an insurmountable objection against the sacrament of penance as being immediately instituted by Christ, since many external aspects of this sacrament have changed through the ages.

It is evident, however, that this problem of historic change has wider ramifications. With the exception of baptism and the Eucharist, whose essence was explicitly determined by Christ in Holy Scripture, the external rites of practically all the sacraments of the New Law have undergone change. The rite of confirmation has certainly undergone an evolution from the primi-

---

[1] This truth was formally defined by the Council of Trent. Cf. H. Lennerz, "Salva Illorum Substantia," in *Gregorianum*, III (1922), 385–419, who says: "The Council of Trent defined that Christ immediately instituted the sacraments against heretics who affirmed that some sacraments were not instituted by Christ, but arose later in the Church." This latter statement is not accepted by all Catholic theologians.

[2] For much of this section see Bernard Leeming, *Principles of Sacramental Theology*, 3 ed. (Westminster, Md. 1960), pp. 385–431.

tive imposition of hands to the anointing; the sacrament of holy orders has shifted from the giving over of the instruments and back once again to the imposition of hands.[3] The problem is obviously not restricted to the sacrament of penance, even though it poses difficulty here as well. After the authoritative articles of De Guibert[4] and Galtier,[5] most theologians agreed that there have been some rather radical changes in the sacraments over the ages. The Church herself in her *Decree for the Armenians* admits this in regard to the change in the requirements for the valid reception of holy orders. "The facts make it hard to deny that the Church did introduce a substantial change in the rite of the Sacrament of Orders, though, of course, not in the substance of the sacrament."[6] But once again the difficult problem of what is the real "substance" of the sacrament arises. All changes introduced into the rite must leave the meaning of the sacrament intact; if they do this, the "substance" of the sacrament has remained unchanged. This latter statement, however, remains to be proven.

Our objective is to set forth the notion and meaning of a sacrament in Catholic doctrine. For this, the principal doctrinal thinker is St. Thomas Aquinas. For even if the Council of Trent did not explicitly endorse the doctrine of any one school, it remains beyond any shadow of a doubt "that only the fundamental perspectives of Thomistic theology, taken up in several documents of the magisterium, can alone render account of all the aspects of ecclesial penance."[7] This present study leads to the

---

[3] See J. Coppens, *L'Imposition des Mains et les Rites Connexes dans le Nouveau Testament et dans l'Église Ancienne* (Louvain, 1925), pp. 25–63; Pius XII, *Constitutio Apostolica Sacramenti Ordinis* (Nov. 30, 1947), AAS, 40 (1948), 5–7 (D.B. 3001); Th. Deman, *Aux Origines de la Théologie Morale* (Montreal, 1951), pp. 14–17; Leeming, op. cit., pp. 394–395; S. Tromp, *De Revelatione*, 5 ed. (Rome, 1945), pp. 316–317.

[4] J. De Guibert, "Le Decret du Concile de Florence pour les Armeniens, sa Valeur Dogmatique," in *Bulletin de Litterature Ecclesiastique*, 10 (1919), 81–95, 150–162.

[5] P. Galtier, article, "Imposition des Mains," in *DTC*, Vol. VII, c. 1411 ff.

[6] B. Leeming, op. cit., p. 421.

[7] P. Anciaux, *Le Sacrément de la Pénitence* (Louvain, 1960), p. 115.

same conclusion with regard to the origin and meaning of the notion of sacrament itself.[8]

I. STATEMENT OF THE PROBLEM

That God alone could institute and give efficacy to all the sacraments of the Church is a fact that no theologian can deny. In the institutions of the New Law, therefore, Christ had to establish the means by which He wished all men to participate in the salvation which He accomplished once and for all on the cross of Calvary. These graces could have been communicated directly without any need of sacraments. As the late Holy Father Pius XII recently explained: "It was possible for Him personally, immediately, to impart these graces to men; but He wished to do so only through a visible Church that would be formed by the union of men."[9] In other words, the Holy Father tells us that God wished to respect the divine economy of creation and redemption in communicating the fruits of salvation: visibility of the Church and of her sacraments.[10] These sacraments are part of the fundamental constitution of the Church as established and settled by Christ Himself. The reality of the sacraments is directly the work of Christ and not of the Apostles or even of the Church. They are her instruments, an extension of the salvation in her bosom; yet they cannot be her creation but must come directly from her divine founder and supporter, Jesus Christ. The reason for this is obvious: grace is a participation in God's own life and being; and, therefore, it can be only God who establishes the means whereby this life can be communicated. This aspect of the institution of the sacraments by Christ is disputed by no Christian theologian.

The difficulty, however, lies in how Christ instituted the

---

[8] For the text of St. Thomas (III, q. 60–65) we have used that reconstructed and commented on by A. M. Roguet, *Les Sacrements* (ed. de la Revue des Jeunes, Paris, 1951).

[9] *Mystici Corporis Christi* (ed. of the Paulist Press), Chap. 13.

[10] See above, Chapter VIII.

sacraments. For some of the sacraments, the answer is quite obvious, since Scripture itself gives us the account of their direct institution by Christ. Baptism and the Holy Eucharist were clearly and directly instituted by Christ. But how did Christ institute the other sacraments of the New Law? The subject of our study, the sacrament of penance, poses some very delicate problems in this respect. The external rite of this sacrament has evolved over the centuries from a more-or-less public penance and reconciliation to a more-or-less private penance and reconciliation. What did Christ institute which is so essential that without it there can be no sacrament of penance? To determine this is especially difficult, if we note that it could not have been the public or private character of the sacrament, since this element has varied during the course of history. What, then, remains constant and unchanging in this sacrament so that in both the private and public forms of penance we can say that it derives from the fundamental institution of Christ?

The Council of Trent in its twenty-first session had this to say of the problem in general: "The Church has always possessed the power, in her dispensation of the sacraments, ever keeping their substance intact — *salva illorum substantia* — to establish or to change, in view of variation of circumstances, time and place, whatever she judges expedient in the interest of the faithful and the reverence due to the sacraments."[11] The Fathers of the Council defended this aspect of change against the Greeks, who claimed that the reception of Holy Communion under one species instead of two changed the fundamental institution of Christ.[12] The Council, then, teaches and distinguishes between the historical aspects of the sacrament (language, formula, prayers, vestments, ceremonies, etc.), which can be changed according to the time and place, according to the needs of the faithful, and the "substance" of the sacrament which cannot be changed

---

[11] Sess. XXI, Chap. 2 (D.B. 931).

[12] For an account of the Council's discussion in this matter see H. Jedin, *Geschichte des Konzils von Trient,* Band II (Verlag Herder, 1960), pp. 153–187.

since it was established by Christ. Pius XII made the same statement with regard to the variation of the rite of sacred ordination to the priesthood: "In the course of the centuries the Church did not and could not substitute other sacraments in place of those instituted by Christ our Lord. The reason is that the seven sacraments of the New Law were all instituted by Jesus Christ our Lord, as the Council of Trent teaches . . . and the Church has no authority over the 'substance of the sacraments,' that is, over the elements that Christ Our Lord Himself, according to the testimony of divine revelation (*ea quae testibus divinae revelationis fontibus ipse Christus in signo sacramentali servanda statuit*), determined what should be kept in the sacramental sign. . . ."[13]

The Council of Trent did not define exactly what this "substance" of the sacraments was, and there has been a rather sharp difference among theologians on this point.[14] The sacraments are universally held to be of divine institution subject to no "substantial" change. Whatever a sacrament is (its essential structure), all theologians agree that Christ established at least this. He determined the essence of each sacrament, no matter how one conceives of this "essence" or "substance."

Yet, the above-cited paragraph of Pius XII gives an insight into this essential structure, the "essence" of what the sacraments are. The Holy Father explained that the substance of the sacrament is precisely that, in the *sacramental sign*, which we know

---

[13] Pius XII, *op. cit.*, D.B. 2301.

[14] B. Leeming, *op. cit.*, pp. 396–431; see the abundance of periodical literature in this field. A. D'Alès, "Salva Eorum Substantia," in *Eph. Théo. Lov.*, I (1924), 297–304; F. Cavallera, "Le Decret du Concile de Trente sur les Sacrements en General," in *Bull. Litt. Eccl.*, 6 (1914), 407–417; H. Dondaine, "Substantia Sacramenti," in *Revue des Sciences Phil. et Théo.*, 29 (1940), 328–335; S. Harent, "Le Part de l'Église dans la Détermination du Rite Sacramentel," in *Etudes*, 73 (1897), 315–336; E. Hugueny, "L'Institution des Sacrements," in *Rev. de Sc. Phil. et Théo.*, 8 (1914), 236–257; A. Boyer, "À Propos de 'Salva Illorum Substantia,'" in *Div. Thom.*, 42 (1953), 38–67; G. R. Smith, "The Church and Her Sacraments," in *Clergy Review*, 33 (1950), 216–232; J. Umberg, "Die Bedeutung des Tridentinischen 'Salva Illorum Substantia,'" in *Zeitschrift für Kath. Theo.*, 48 (1924), 161–195, etc.

from Scripture or Tradition to have been instituted by Christ.
Not only do those who hold that the essence of the sacraments
may be embodied in different rites have less historical difficulties,
but they also have, it would seem, the same view as that of the
Holy Father himself. In other words, without going into any
detailed study of the history of the expressions, "substance" or
"essential qualities" of a sacrament, it is necessary to search for
a solution to the problem along the lines of the sacrament's
signification and *meaning*, as the Holy Father has pointed out.
A short history of the constitutive elements of a sacrament in
the writings of the Fathers and a detailed study of the sacramental doctrine of St. Thomas Aquinas will provide a satis-
factory solution to this problem. The method is legitimate and
necessary since, as the Holy Father has pointed out, the essential
elements of a sacrament can be determined from a study of the
divine fonts of revelation (Scripture and Tradition). But since
so little can be adduced directly from Scripture to solve this
problem (outside of baptism and the Eucharist), it is impera-
tive to make a short study of sacramental evolution in the history
of the Church. Only in this way will we see what Tradition says
about the evolution of the sacraments and what it considered to
be the essential qualities of the sacraments.

II. Short Historical Survey[15]

As early as the apostolic period, St. John the Evangelist saw
the sacraments as instituted by Christ on the cross and issuing
symbolically from His wounded side. Patristic Tradition witnesses
to the same understanding of the origins of the sacraments of
the Church. That only Christ could have instituted these means
of salvation was so much a part of that tradition that no special

15 D. J. Kennedy, art. "Sacraments," in *The Catholic Encyclopedia*, Vol.
XIII, pp. 290–310; see also A. Michel, "Matière et Forme," in *DTC*, Vol. X,
col. 346–349; H. Dondaine, "La Definition des Sacrements dans la Somme
Théologique," in *Rev. des Sc. Phi. et Théo.*, 31 (1947), 214–228; E.
Doronzo, *Tractatus Dogmaticus de Sacramentis in Genere* (Milwaukee,
1946), pp. 400–418.

mention was even made of it; it was simply taken for granted both by Christian and heretic alike.

It is likewise true that, during the earliest Patristic period, a twofold aspect was attributed to every sacramental rite. There is always some visible element (*dromenon*) and a spoken element (*legomenon*). Tertullian, St. Cyprian, St. Cyril of Alexandria, St. Irenaeus, St. Gregory of Nyssa, St. Ambrose, and St. Augustine always spoke of the sacraments as constituted of these two elements.[16] All refer to the power of the word, or the blessing, or invocation with regard to some physical element over which these formulae were pronounced.

St. Irenaeus, for example, in his *Adv. Haereses* (IV, 18, 5) tells us: "the bread of the earth, receiving the invocation (*epiclesis*) of God, is no longer common bread, but the Eucharist, consisting of two things, an earthy and a heavenly." For Irenaeus and other early witnesses of the Faith, terrestial things became sacraments because of the power of God, the power of the word of God or the power of the Spirit of God. Through the invocation of the minister (the sacred words used in the sacrament), the word or the Holy Spirit consecrates the things of this earth. Here, then, the *dromenon* (what is done, the terrestrial thing) is sanctified by the *legomenon* (what is said, the words), and the latter is simply the vehicle of God's own power. In the words of St. Augustine with reference to the baptismal rite: "What is the baptism of Christ? A washing in water by the word. Take away the water and you have no baptism; take away the word, and you have no baptism." And again: "And in the water the word cleanses. Take away the word, and what is water but water? The word comes to the element and a sacrament results" (*accedit verbum ad elementum et fit sacramentum*).[17]

In other words, for these early Patristic witnesses, a sacrament

---

[16] See among thousands of texts St. Irenaeus, *Adv. Haereses*, 3, 17, 2 (*P.G.*, 7, c. 930); St. Augustine, *In Joannem*, 11, 11 (*P.L.*, 34, c. 560), *Tract*. 15 n. 4 (*P.L.*, 35, c. 1513); *De Civitate Dei*, 15, 26 (*P.L.*, 41, c. 472); St. Cyril of Jerusalem, *Cat.*, 3; St. Ambrose, *In Luc.*, 10, 35 (*P.L.*, 15, c. 1938); St. Cyril of Alexandria, *In Joan.*, 1, 12 (*P.G.*, 74, c. 677); etc.

[17] *Tract* 15 *in Joanneum* (*P.L.*, 35, c. 1512).

is a terrestrial thing consecrated by the power of the word of
God. Things so consecrated are no longer earthy because they
have been consecrated and sanctified by the word which is the
vehicle of God's power. For just as the Incarnate Word sanctified His flesh and deified His humanity by its assumption by
the Word, so now in the visible sacraments, God sanctifies earthy
things and uses them to convey His sanctifying powers to men.
"It is clear that in their minds [the Fathers], there are in a
sacrament two things, the material element and the verbal."[18]
These ancient Fathers considered two things as absolutely essential for the existence of a sacrament (what we would call its
"substance"): a material element and words. They held that
both constituted a sacrament. There certainly are no explicit
texts in the Fathers telling us that they considered these two
elements as "essential," but the fact remains that when they
speak of sacrament they *always* mention these two elements as
constituting the "inner core" or the sacramental reality — what
we call its substance, since, in the words of St. Augustine, one
without the other cannot bring about the sacramental reality.
Care must be taken, however, not to see in these two elements
what the later scholastic authors termed "matter" and "form."
These later terms with regard to the sacraments will be worked
out in an entirely different theological context. These elements
shall be examined later.

To be absolutely correct, there were *three* elements in the
early Fathers' doctrine on the sacraments: the terrestrial element,
the invocative word, and, finally, the power of God which is invoked by the word (the prayer or *epiclesis*). The word is simply
the vehicle for this power of God, which alone transforms the
terrestrial elements into heavenly elements. St. Justin Martyr, in
his first *Apologia*, refers to all three elements when speaking of
the Eucharist: the terrestrial element, the words, and the power
of God. ". . . the food which has been made the Eucharist by
the prayer of His Word, and which nourishes our flesh and blood

---

[18] Leeming, *op. cit.*, p. 404.

by assimilation, is both the flesh and blood of that Jesus who was made flesh."[19] Clement of Alexandria writes that in the sacrament of the Eucharist, there is an *invocation* to the Holy Spirit, and hence by the power of the Holy Spirit the bread and the wine (the terrestial elements) become the body and the blood of Christ. St. Cyril of Jerusalem has the same teaching: ". . . the bread and wine of the Eucharist, before the sacred invocation (*Epiclesis*) of the adorable Trinity, was ordinary bread and wine, but, after the invocation, the bread becomes the body of Christ, and the wine the blood of Christ."[20] St. Gregory of Nyssa also teaches exactly the same doctrine: "Rightly do we believe that now also the bread which is consecrated by the Word of God is made over into the body of God the Word. . . . In this case the bread, as the Apostle says, is consecrated by means of the word and prayer; not that it advances by the process of eating into becoming the body of the Word, but it is at once made over into the body by means of the Word, as the Word said, 'This is my body.' . . ."[21] And finally the words of St. Ambrose: "Now if the word of Elias was powerful enough to bring down fire from heaven, will not the words of Christ be powerful enough to change the specific nature of the eucharistic elements?"[22]

For both the Latin and the Greek Fathers, the essence of a sacrament consists in the consecration by God, who can sanctify everything just as He had the power to create everything from nothing. This consecration of the terrestrial elements is brought about by the words of the minister which act as the necessary vehicle of the divine power. This last element is called fittingly the *epiclesis* by the Greeks, or the *invocation* or *calling down*. This "calling down" is a direct reference to the fact that the

---

[19] *The First Apology* (tr. T. Falls, *Saint Justin Martyr*, The Fathers of the Church, ed. Schopp), pp. 100–101.

[20] *On the Mysteries*, 1, 7 (*Florilegium Patristium*, ed. Geyer-Zellinger) as quoted in P. Palmer, *Sources of Christian Theology*, I, *Sacraments and Worship* (Westminster, Md., 1955), p. 137.

[21] *Catechetical Oration*, 37 (P.G., 45, c. 93).

[22] *On the Mysteries*, 4 (*Florilegium Patristium*, 100–104).

necessary words are the means which God uses to change the
simple terrestrial elements which are before our eyes.

In the witness of the Latin Fathers, particularly in that of St.
Ambrose and above all in that of St. Augustine, a sacrament consists of the union of the two elements — the terrestrial and the
word, and this union is achieved through the power of God.
For St. Augustine, however, the word has a very special meaning
and must be taken into careful consideration, since from the
time of the reformers, St. Augustine's doctrine on the Real
Presence has been greatly criticized. In the Middle Ages, sacramental realism, especially of the Eucharist, had been exaggerated
by some almost to the point of cannibalism. In the Reforma-
tion period, idealism or the "spiritual" interpretation of the
Eucharist passages of the New Testament resulted in the denial
of the Real Presence itself.[23] Some of the main arguments adduced against the Catholic position were drawn from St. Augustine.[24] In any case, a study of the use of "word" in St. Augustine
will clarify this controversy.

For St. Augustine the main reason why the word uttered over
the element is efficacious in producing the divine result is that
the word is the word of Christ Himself (Verbum Verbi). It is
thus the heavenly word, the celestial word which (like the word
of God in the beginning in Gn 1:1) brings forth what it says.
The word of Christ, then, causes divine effects since it is the
very word of God the Son. The second reason for the efficaciousness of the word is that it is the word of faith. This is principally from the Church's point of view which has its faith in
Christ. In speaking of baptism once again, St. Augustine says:
"Whence this power of water so exalted as to bathe the body
and cleanse the soul, if it is not through the action of the word;
not because it is spoken, but because it is believed? . . . This
word of faith is of such efficacy in the Church of God that it

---

[23] P. Palmer, op. cit., p. 141.

[24] For the controversial texts of St. Augustine, see Commentary on Ps. 98
(P.L., 37, c. 1264–1265); Sermo 131 (P.L., 38, c. 729); Commentarium in
Joannem, 27, 5 (P.L., 35, c. 1617); De Civitate Dei, 10, 6, 20 (P.L.,
41, c. 281–290); and parallel passages.

washes clean not only the one who believes in the word, the one who presents (the child for Baptism), the one who sprinkles (the child), but the child itself, be it ever so tiny, even though it is as yet incapable of believing unto justice. . . ."[25] In other words, our faith or the faith of the Church makes it a reality for us, an efficacious means of salvation for us. Without this faith, even the omnipotent power of God is helpless to make us believe. We believe in the word of Christ and we believe in the power of God present in the word. Hence, in the sacraments, there is an expression of faith by which we participate in Christ. In a very true sense, a sacrament is the expression of faith in the all-powerful word of Christ who has revealed that what He says He can do. St. Augustine certainly does not wish to imply that it is man's faith which brings about the conversion, say, of simple bread into the body of Christ. All he is attempting to expound is the traditional Catholic doctrine that God's saving sacraments cannot save him who does not believe in God's word.

The tradition of the two-element theory of the sacraments had a further development in a manner that was not traditional. The early scholastic theologians (1000–1200), such as Peter Lombard, speak in a traditional fashion of the two elements of the sacraments. While it is true that in the course of time the terrestrial elements of bread and wine in the Eucharist were called variously the likeness, antitype, representation, sacrament, or figure of Christ's body, still the tradition of the early Middle Ages was very much similar to that of the early Fathers of the Church. Hylomorphism was not as yet in vogue. Some of the Fathers, however, had spoken of the "form" of the sacrament. Tertullian, for example, speaks of the *forma praescripta*. For him, however, the meaning of "form" had nothing to do with the "form" as later introduced under the influence of Aristotelian terminology. It simply meant or designated the official or pre-

---

[25] *Treatise on the Gospel of St. John*, 80, 3 (P.L., 35, c. 1840). As Palmer remarks (*op. cit.*, p. 87, footnote 1) we must not conclude from this passage that the efficacy of baptism depends solely on the subjective faith of the one who is baptized, since the baptism of infants presupposes that they have no subjective faith.

scribed rite which consisted of the res and the verba of the sacrament (i.e., the terrestrial element and the words as presented in
all of the early Fathers). The material element, as described by
the Fathers, cannot be called the "prime matter" of Aristotle's
matter and form. It meant simply the material element man
can see, touch, and taste. Some scholastic terms are therefore
used by the Fathers but without any of the later scholastic
meanings.

It is difficult to say exactly when the Aristotelian terminology
of "matter" and "form" was first applied to the sacraments. The
first to apply such a terminology was probably Stephen Langton
(1228), although William of Auxerre also used it at about the
same time.[26] In any case, its use became prevalent in the West
after the introduction of Aristotle into Christian circles during
the latter part of the twelfth century and the beginning of the
thirteenth. Many of the early scholastics of this period saw the
two elements of "matter" and "form" used in the Fathers and
read Aristotelian meanings into them. The beginnings of hylomorphism in connection with the sacraments, then, belongs to
this period. In Aristotelian philosophy, "matter" was a principle
of extension, indeterminate in itself, whereas "form" was a principle of unity, determination, and specification. It is easy to see
how this theory gained the approval of most of the scholastic
theologians of the period.

The great scholastics of the thirteenth century, however,
showed some judicious use of this terminology when they applied it to the sacraments of the New Law. St. Thomas' use
of this terminology was tempered and wise. In regard to "matter" and "form," St. Thomas consistently qualifies their use by
"in a way" (per modum) or "almost" (quasi).[27] He concedes
that the element (e.g., bread) can be called matter, although
it is not prime matter in the strict sense. The essential genius

26 A. Michel, article "Matière et Forme," in D.T.C., Vol. X, c. 346–349;
Leeming, op. cit., pp. 404–405.
27 See III, q. 60, a. 7, in Corpore: "in sacramentis verba se habent per
modum formae, res autem sensibiles per modum materiae."

of St. Thomas lies in the fact that his whole sacramental system is not based primarily on "matter" and "form" (although these two elements are essential for St. Thomas), but on their *signification*. Matter and form in this context are united only inasmuch as they express one signification. The words, for example, are defined as *signs* and not as *things*. They pertain to the essence of the sacrament not by their materiality but by their signification.[28] This qualification on this point is important because so much sacramental theology has been influenced by this terminology.[29] Cardinal Franzelin rightly warns against a too philosophical interpretation of this division of the sacraments:

> In physical things, the matter and form make up a composite thing, physically one; but in the sacraments there only arises one signification, from the matter conveying the meaning less expressly, and the form more determinately, and hence the unity is the unity of a sign. For this, a merely moral conjunction of the matter and form is sufficient, so that, according to the estimation of men, for whose sake the sign was instituted, both elements concur to make up one signification. But exactly what conjunction and simultaneity in the placing of the matter and form is needful to produce this unity of a sign must be judged in each sacrament. . . .[30]

St. Thomas avoided such pitfalls in terminology and materiality of formulation in his brilliant exposition of the nature of the sacramental system. This will be the subject matter of the following section.

---

[28] A. M. Roguet, *op. cit.*, p. 211; see St. Thomas, III, q. 60, a. 8, ad 3; a. 6, ad 2.

[29] *Ibid.*, p. 210; Leeming, *op. cit.*, p. 405.

[30] J. B. Franzelin, *Tractatus de Sacramentis*, 3 ed. (Rome, 1881), p. 38. An orthodox theologian has also noticed this danger in Western terminology with regard to the sacraments: "This visible part which the ancient Fathers called a visible sign and Tertullian called *res*, the Westerns from the 13th Century subdivided, according to Aristotle, into matter and form . . . this distinction which is also to be found in our own dogmatical and catechetical books, is unnecessary and unreliable. . . . Unnecessary because it was unknown to the undivided Church, and yet did not in any way affect the working of the means of grace." C. Androutsos, *The Validity of English Ordinations from an Orthodox Point of View* (Athens, 1903), p. 68.

III. The Doctrine of St. Thomas on
the Sacraments

St. Thomas' doctrine on the sacraments is contained in the
third part of the *Summa Theologiae* and follows in logical order
after the part concerning the Word Incarnate. The sacraments,
in fact, serve as the direct communication and application of
the merits and graces of the Word Incarnate. St. Thomas explicitly said this.[31] The sacraments are nothing more than the
communication of Christ Himself and channels of His grace.
They are also the means of the Christian cult which permit man
once again to advance toward God in and through Christ. They
are, above all, the primary and most important acts of the Christian priesthood. Especially pertinent in this context is question
60 of the third part in which St. Thomas exposes his doctrine on
the sacraments.

In the first article, St. Thomas asks whether the sacraments are
even signs at all. He replies in the affirmative and uses a comparison to bring out his point:

> All things that are ordained to one, even in different ways,
> can be nominated from it; thus, from health which is in an
> animal, not only is the animal said to be healthy through being
> the subject of health: but medicine also is said to be healthy
> through producing health; diet through preserving it; and urine
> through being a sign of health. Consequently, a thing may be
> called a sacrament, either from having a certain hidden sanctity,
> and in this sense a sacrament is a sacred secret, or as having
> some relationship to this sanctity, which relationship may be that
> of a cause, or of a sign or of any other relation. But now we are
> speaking of sacraments in a special sense, as implying the relation-
> ship of sign, and in this way, a sacrament is a kind of sign.[32]

St. Thomas is obviously using an analogy of attribution applied
to different things according to different relationships. Here St.
Thomas explains that the sacraments are essentially signs because they have a relationship to the thing signified, which, in

---

[31] II[a] II[ae], q. 89.
[32] III, q. 60, a. 1, *in Corpore*.

this case, is sanctity. Formally, it is not so much the matter of the sign that counts but the signification that the matter takes from the thing which it signifies. It is from the relationship to the thing signified that the sign draws its signification. The sacrament is not to be considered as a thing so much as a sign; it is not to be considered as a physical thing in its visible elements, but must be considered formally, that is, insofar as it signifies sanctity or a sacred thing. The material reality contains a signification which the words determine and complete (more on this point later).

In the second article in this same question the thought of St. Thomas progresses further on the signification of the sacrament. He asks whether every sign of a holy thing is a sacrament. St. Thomas replies in the negative saying: "A sacrament properly so called is that which is the sign of some sacred thing pertaining to man; so that properly speaking a sacrament, as considered by us now, is defined as being *the sign* of a holy thing in so far as it makes man holy."[33] St. Thomas argues in this article that not all signs of sacred things are sacraments but only those signs of sacred things which actually sanctify men (*signum efficax gratiae*). A sacrament is, therefore, not an ordinary sign since this sacramental sign both signifies sacred things and also brings about the sanctity of man. There are signs in nature which serve to instruct the mind about a deeper meaning. Such is the case with figures and allegories, but they cannot be called sacraments properly speaking. Sacraments instruct the mind of man, but they also sanctify by signifying. By their signification, the sacraments instruct on the realities and truths of faith; but on the other hand, they demand, from those who so view them, a true profession of faith which also can produce a living faith.

This argument of the efficacy of the sacraments through their signification is further strengthened in the reply to the second objection. Christian Tradition has always held that there were

---

[33] III, q. 60, a. 2, *in Corpore*. Italics mine. See also the second objection in this same article.

true sacraments in the Old Testament. How can this be reconciled with the dogma of the Christian faith that the efficacy of all the sacraments is derived from the passion and death of Christ? The answer is clear if argued along the lines of their signification. The elements (paschal lamb, circumcision, etc.) of the Old Testament were nothing more than the protestation of faith in the coming Savior; those of the New Law are protestations of faith in the passion and death of Christ. Those of the Old Law were directed toward Christ who was to come; those of the new are directed toward Christ who has come and continues to save us.

In the third article St. Thomas develops the traditional theme that each sacrament has a threefold signification.

> A sacrament properly so called is that which is ordained to signify our sanctification. Three things may be considered here: the cause of our sanctification, which is the passion of Christ; the form of our sanctification, which consists of grace and the virtues; and the ultimate end of our sanctification, which is eternal life. All these three things are signified by the sacraments. Hence, a sacrament is a commemorative sign of that which preceded it which is the passion of Christ; a demonstrative sign of that which is effected in us by Christ's passion which is grace; and a prognostic sign because it foretells our future glory.[34]

Our sanctification, then, can be considered in three ways. One is the most fundamental, and this is the passion of Christ. The other two are secondary because they are the effect and final end of the first.

It is extremely unfortunate that this brilliant doctrine on the efficacy of the sacraments was more or less lost by later scholastics and especially by the Nominalists. St. Thomas was in the tradition of all the Fathers of the Church when he qualified Aristotelian hylomorphism as applied both to the sensible elements and to the word. Later scholastics, who considered the sacraments more from their material point of view than from their signification, seem to have taken the Aristotelian formula too

---

[34] III, q. 60, a. 3, *in Corpore*. See in this regard the threefold aspect of the sacrament of the Eucharist in the *Sacrum Convivium* of St. Thomas.

literally. A. Michel concludes his study on the tradition of matter and form in the scholastics by saying: "all Thomists generally teach that the subject, to which is attached the sacramental signification, includes, *as an a priori condition of that signification*, a real composition between the formal element and the material element."[35] This judgment is incorrect in view of the teaching of St. Thomas. He does not primarily consider the sacraments as physical things but as *signs*. For St. Thomas, a sacrament is above all a sign.

Yet, for all this, St. Thomas considers that the sensible elements in sacraments are essential to their constitution. In the fourth article of this same question, he gives a double reason for the necessity of the material or sensible element in the sacrament.

> Divine wisdom provides for each being according to its own nature. . . . It is in the nature of man to come to the knowledge of intelligible things by means of the sensible. A sign, on the other hand, is a means of arriving at the knowledge of something else. Therefore, the sacred things which the sacraments ought to signify, being spiritual and intelligible things by which man sanctifies himself, it is only by means of sensible elements that a sacrament will be fully a sign.[36]

Hence, St. Thomas argues from the essential composite which man is. A unit of body and soul, man requires by his nature that spiritual gifts come to him through material signs because God saves man in the manner in which He created him. The nature of St. Thomas' thought is further developed in the second and third objections of this article. The objection is that God is a Spirit and that those who adore Him must do so in spirit. Therefore, material things are not required for the sacraments. St. Thomas answers that the sensible elements considered in their own natures do not belong to the Kingdom of God; they must be considered only as *signs* of spiritual things of which the Kingdom of God consists. This response once again brings out the fact that St. Thomas considers the sensible elements of the sacra-

---

[35] *Art. cit.*, Vol. X, c. 340. Italics mine.
[36] III, q. 60, art. 4, *in Corpore*.

ments important and necessary, but not according to their physical being, but as a kind of sign.

In the fifth article, St. Thomas continues the notion of the sacraments as signs. A sign is a relation added to the being of a thing. Different things could, conceivably, signify different things. Therefore, a multitude of things could be used by God or man in accomplishing the act of cult. Although this is true, it must be remembered that a sacrament in the New Law is an efficacious sign; it joins man to the sanctity of God by its sanctification.

> In the use of sacraments, two things must be considered: the worship of God and the sanctification of man. The first of these belongs to man in reference to God and the second belongs to God in reference to man. Now it is not for everyone to determine that which is in the power of the other. Therefore, since the sanctification of man is in the power of God who sanctifies, it is not up to man to decide what things should be used for his sanctification; rather this is decided by divine institution. Therefore, in the sacraments of the New Law by which men are sanctified . . . we must use those things which are determined by divine institution.[37]

The important thing brought out in this article is that in the sacraments, once again, it is not so much the materiality of the elements which is important, but their signification. But since the signification comes from God, it is up to Him to determine what it shall be. It is true that St. Thomas lacked the historical perspectives that are available today. Certain material elements in the sacraments, for example, have changed in the course of the ages, and therefore St. Thomas erred in saying that God has explicitly determined the sensible elements of the sacraments. But this makes little difference to his fundamental principle. The material elements in the sacraments (matter and form) pertain to the essence of the sacraments not by their materiality but by their signification. "The words have above all (*principaliter*) the value of sign," as Thomas says.[38]

---

[37] III, q. 60, art. 5, *in Corpore.*

[38] It is clear that in this conception of Catholic doctrine, every reproach of magic is, by that very fact, completely silenced.

St. Thomas proceeds to the most important aspect of the sensible elements in the sacraments: the words that, as in the patristic tradition, are both the vehicles of God's life and the protestation of man's faith. St. Thomas asks whether words are necessary in the sacraments. He answers in the affirmative and does so for a threefold reason: from the part of God, of man, and of the signification of the material element itself. The symbolism of things is in the purely natural order, and it is principally by the words that the signification is transferred to the supernatural order. From the part of God, "the sacraments can be considered in regard to the cause of sanctification, the Word Incarnate, to whom the sacraments have a certain conformity in that the word is joined to the sensible thing just as in the mystery of the Incarnation the Word of God is united to sensible flesh."[39] The structure of the sacraments is therefore like the structure of the very being of the God-Man. This whole question presupposes the doctrine of St. Thomas (cf. *supra*, Chap. VIII, p. 124 ff) on the humanity of Christ; He performed miracles through His humanity but in virtue of His divinity (i.e., the hypostatic union), and on this analogy St. Thomas draws a comparison with reference to the sacraments. The material elements in the sacraments become the instrument of divine power.

Then St. Thomas considers the words from the point of view of man: "The sacraments may be considered in regard to man who is sanctified, and who is composed of body and soul; to him the sacramental remedy is fitted since it touches the body through the sensible element, and the soul through faith in the words."[40] Here St. Thomas is in full patristic tradition by arguing from "the word of faith." It is not so much the spoken word that matters but faith in those words (i.e., their full signification as *believed*). It is not by pronunciation that the word reaches the soul, but by faith. A word is certainly a sensible thing, but it is not by that virtue that words are operative in the sacraments. Otherwise, they would be nothing more than magic formulae.

[39] III, q. 60, art. 6, *in Corpore.*
[40] *Ibid.*

"What is important in them is their signification, which is addressed both to the intelligence and to faith."[41]

Finally, the words are considered from the point of view of the signification itself:

> The sacraments can be considered in regard to their signification. St. Augustine remarks that words are the principal signs used by men: because words can be formed in various ways for the purpose of signifying various concepts, so that we are able to express our thoughts with greater distinctness by means of words. And, therefore, in order to insure the perfection of the sacramental signification it was necessary for the signification of sensible things to be determined by words. For water can signify both a cleansing because of its wetness, and refreshment because of its coolness: but when *Ego te baptizo* is said, it is clear that the water is used in Baptism to signify a spiritual cleansing.[42]

Words, then, belong to the form of the sacrament because of the sense signified by them.[43] For St. Thomas, words are the most precise kind of signs which are required by a sacrament which is itself a sign. The sensible element and the words are not added as two beings to one nature, but as complementing each other in the order of signification. "The sensible elements begin a signification that the word determines, completes, and defines."[44]

The priority of words over the material elements, however, is an important aspect of Thomistic doctrine. Words are *of themselves* signs and do not exist except insofar as they signify. A word is useless unless it signifies something. On the other hand, material things can have other meanings, as St. Thomas points out with regard to water. Psychologically speaking, words make the signification of things more precise and make material things signify but one thing. Theologically speaking, words serve to raise the symbolism of material things to the supernatural plane. In baptism, for example, the water signifies a spiritual

---

[41] A. M. Roguet, *op. cit.*, p. 209: the famous expression of St. Augustine: "*Verbum non ut dicitur sed ut creditur.*"

[42] III, q. 60, art. 6.

[43] *Ibid.*

[44] Roguet, *op. cit.*, p. 210.

cleansing because of the accompanying words. What is signified in the words used is the object of the Church's faith. Likewise, St. Thomas says in his *Commentary on the Four Books of Sentences:* "The forms of the sacraments are professions of faith."[45] The words, finally, give efficacy to the sacrament. Not only do they signify but they *effect what they signify:* "The form of the words is the means by which efficacy comes to the matter which is sanctified by them."[46] They are efficacious because they are the words of Christ and are the vehicles of Christ's redemptive passion and death.

St. Thomas, then, is far from holding the hylomorphic theory of later scholastics. His doctrine, profoundly traditional, strongly developed the sacraments as signs. For St. Thomas, the signification is the form of the sacraments: the matter is composed of all the externals: both the words (*quasi forma*) and the material element (*quasi materia*).

IV. Various Opinions on the "Substance" of the Sacraments

The original question still remains: What is "substantial" and what is "accidental" in the sacraments? In other words, what did Christ institute so that if it be taken away, the sacrament would cease to exist? Most Catholic authors are agreed that some change has taken place in most of the sacraments, and there are very few who hold that there is no evidence for any change in the form of the sacraments. It is hard to see how such a theory could be held in light of historical evidence. Nevertheless, A. Michel claims that two Salamanca theologians, Gonet and Billiart, held this theory, and Doronzo in our day holds that "Christ more probably instituted all the sacraments not merely in a generic manner but in a specific manner."[47]

---

[45] D. 3, a. 2, ad 4. See also III, q. 60, a. 8, ad 2.
[46] *Ibid.*, D. 3, q. 1, a. 3; sol. 3, ad 2; *De Articulis Fidei et Ecclesiae*, Chap. 6.
[47] *Op. cit.*, p. 408, as quoted in Leeming, *op. cit.*, p. 413.

To explain the historical changes that have taken place in the course of time, many authors have recourse to the generic manner of institution. This maintains that Christ settled the meaning of the sacrament, but left power with the Apostles or the Church to determine the elements in which this meaning may be embodied.[48] Thus the essential of the sacrament would remain the same as long as the signification which Christ intended could aptly be embodied in a diverse number of material elements or rites. In other words, these authors hold that Christ could have instituted all the sacraments without any specific determination of the rite. These authors rightly argue that the institution and essence of a sacrament is giving efficacy to a sign and that a sign is formally made such by its signification. Thus marriage as a sacrament signifies the love between Christ and the Church and the indissoluble union as its main property. But the substantial meaning and signification is not changed if the manner in which the consent between the two parties is changed, say, in giving and accepting gifts. For these authors, then, it does not seem essential that Christ should have determined more than the substantial meaning of the sacrament. In this study of penance it seems reasonable, in view of the changes in the Church's practice in using the power of the keys, to hold that Christ instituted the sacrament as any legitimate manifestation of the Church's judgment and fixed no specific rite. Monsigneur Coppens concludes the discussion of this theory by saying "that the studies made by Harent, DeBaets, Schmidt, Mangenot, De Guibert, Galtier, Cavallera, Lennerz, and D'Ales have definitely demonstrated that the Council of Trent did not wish to refer to Christ the specific determination of the matter and form of the sacraments."[49] Leeming concludes that what is the "substance" of each sacrament must be learned from a study of the individual sacrament.

A. Michel considers every physical thing as being composed of

---

[48] Among these authors one would cite Peter de Soto, Ruard Tapper, Lugo, Hurter, Gotti, Billot, De Smet, Van Noort, Tanquerey, Coppens, D'Ales.

[49] J. Coppens, *op. cit.*, p. 404.

matter and form. Since the sacraments are primarily material
things, they are also composed of matter and form, the matter
being the material thing, and the form, the words. Unfortu-
nately, he considers this aspect of the sacraments even before he
examines the signification of the sacraments. Since, therefore, the
matter and form constitute the essence of a thing, the essence of
the sacraments is their matter and form. The crux of the problem lies in trying to explain the historical difficulties which such
a theory encounters. We have already pointed out that St.
Thomas' thought was qualified when speaking of matter and
form in reference to the sacraments. Even though Thomas erred
in seeing a *de facto* establishment of the matter and form (material element and the words) by Christ, still, and this is very
important, the essential element in the sacraments is the signification which comes from Christ by the economy of the
Incarnation. As a result, even within the context of his quasi
immutable theory, St. Thomas holds that the sacraments can be
accidentally changed provided that their signification is preserved.

Fathers Chenu and Dondaine would hold that the substance
of the sacraments is their signification and that the Church can
change the sacraments provided that she keeps their signification.
This is similar to the theory of the theologians quoted above.
Our historical inquiry proves that this theory is quite insufficient,
since for Tradition it is *not only* the signification that belongs
to the essence of the sacraments but also the fact that the
signification is had in some *material* sign. The Fathers (as well
as St. Thomas) hold that the material element of the sacraments
is a sign which can be distinguished into the sensible element
(matter, rite) and the words. The substance of the sacraments,
therefore, has never been defined by the Church because it is
already found in Tradition. From the examination of Tradition,
salvo meliori judicio, the essence of the sacraments is *both* the
signification manifested in a rite apt to signify it and in words
which aid in expressing that signification. This would seem to be
in all of Tradition since it considers the sacraments as a kind of

sign and includes both the words and the material element in
the sign. A sacrament without a rite would be against all of
Tradition. The rite would seem to be nothing more than an
extension of the economy of the Incarnation in which Christ
acted through His body. The sacraments are signs: thus there is
something with a reference to the signification. This reference
is twofold, the material element and the words. When Christ
did not determine these material things and the words, it is up
to the Church to do so. The Holy Father, Pius XII, did not
alter the state of controversy about the exact manner of Christ's
institution of the sacraments, but he did give an authentic interpretation of the famous Tridentine phrase "*Salva illorum substantia*" in saying that the essence of the sacraments lies in
their signification ("sacramental sign") and the elements ("the
elements that our Lord Himself determined according to the
testimony of divine revelation").[50]

Conclusion

In the sacraments as witnessed in Tradition, two essential
qualities can be distinguished: a transhistorical element (including the essence of the rite), and the words of the sacrament.
The latter can be changed as long as the transhistorical element
remains, but there will always be some form of rite and some
words.

In penance, the transhistorical element will be a judgment by
the Church in reference to sin and its consequent forgiveness of
them in the name of God if the Church judges the penitent
disposed to forgiveness. The historical element will be the accidental features of the rite and the words in which this judgment
is embodied. The public or private way in which this judgment
is exercised makes little difference to the essential. This can be
changed to meet the necessities of God's people of which the
Church is sole judge.

---

[50] G. D. Smith, "The Church and Her Sacraments," in *Clergy Review*,
33 (1950), 223.

General Conclusion

It should be clear to the reader that this small book has not attempted to be a complete study of sin and penance as they are seen in the plan of God's salvation. It was simply an attempt to capture some of the important points of this study. Those who would wish to continue their readings may consult the literature mentioned in the footnotes and in the bibliographical notes (pp. 169–181). Looking back on the work as a whole, one would be tempted not to call it a real book at all but a series of essays on diverse elements in the Christian notion of sin and penance.

Salvation is no mere improvement of the condition of being; it ranks in importance with the creation of all being. It originates not within the structure of the world, not even in the most spiritual part of it, but within the pure freedom of God. This new creation, this new man is a new existence, a new structure, a new being which is created in "the image and justice of God." Man's sin alone can destroy this marvelous gift of God; man's sin is revolt against this divine order, rejection of God's love and friendship given to us in Christ. Sin can only be understood in this personal relationship between God and man. Yet revelation is by nature beyond any complete definition and understanding by men; when faced with it, man must simply be silent and listen. Man has the power, however, to say no to this beckoning of God's love and life; he can reject the blood of Christ shed for him and his sins; he can crush the spark of the divine life in his soul; he can break the bond of personal love between himself and his Creator. This is sin in its full Christian meaning in Holy Scripture. By that revolt, however, man destroys himself in the very marrow of his existence, for one essential composite of his mortal being — so to speak — is his dependency and relationship with the Immortal who is God. The result can only be death and misery of all types. The death of the body, in this context, is but a result of the death of his soul. To reject God (especially as given to us in Christ) by sin is the most repelling evil. God's love for men is manifested in Christ's death for sin: to accept this gift is to have eternal life; to reject it is to enter the depths of black and eternal death. Christ is God's response to man's sin, to man's revolt. In Him alone can men find any hope for the forgiveness of their sins and the promise of eternal life. God has spoken once and forever through the voice and deeds of His only-begotten Son. Man need only respond to this love by his own faith and love.

But man must repair the breach his evil has effected. His internal sentiments (an essential part of true penance) must become manifest in works worthy once again of a son of God; he must perform penance for his deeds, and this is painful and laborious. This penance is described as a "turning" from his sin and directing his ways according to God's will and love for him. A man must put on a new mentality, a change of heart, which can be done only by God's grace and a painful uprooting of past tendencies and pleasures of his sinful ways.

Yet God has not left man alone in this difficult task of Christian penance. He has given man an aid as well as an infallible guarantee of his forgiveness after the sinner has sincerely performed his penance. The sinner's sorrow and penance must be joined to the saving grace of Christ's passion and death, for Christ's grace can alone forgive sin. Where is man to find this saving grace? Only in the Church, for through her alone does Christ continue His salvific work of mercy and forgiveness; He has entrusted all to her in the promise He gave that "whatsoever you shall loose on earth, it shall be loosed in heaven." This grace of forgiveness, this judgment of the sinner is in her hands and in her power. He must come to her if he wishes forgiveness, if he wishes to be united with the saving grace of Christ's passion and death. Thus these three essential elements of penance are united in what we have called ecclesial penance: the part of the sinner who repents; the divine element in the application of the grace of Christ's passion and death; the part of the Church, the Community of Salvation, who receives the sinner and who alone can impart to him the saving graces of Christ through her apostolic ministry. This essential aspect of ecclesial penance, stressed so much by the Fathers of the Church, can be expressed by the technical formula: reconciliation with the Church is the *res et sacramentum* of sacramental penance, that is, it is the sign or pledge of the ultimate effect of the sacrament of penance which is the sacramental grace of God's life. This efficacy of ecclesial penance is founded entirely on the mystery of the Cross of Christ. The remission of sins is entirely the work of God through Christ in the Holy Spirit. The sinner's reconciliation with the Church will be the infallible sign of his forgiveness by God.

No aspect of ecclesial penance can be considered separately: all aspects form one whole in the accomplishment of the destruction of sin. Each one of these essential elements of penance takes on its true signification and value in relation with the other two. The destruction of sin in the sinner is the result of the cooperative efforts of the penitent, God, and the Church united in the one reality called the sacrament of ecclesial penance.

Bibliographical Note

The works cited in this scriptural, historical, and dogmatic sketch of the sacrament of penance are sufficient to show that both technical and popular works on this sacrament are plentiful. Moreover, it is not accidental that the recent Holy Father, Pius XII, in one of his great encyclicals, encouraged the frequent use of this sacrament: ". . . to hasten daily progress along the path of virtue, we wish the pious practice of frequent confession to be earnestly advocated. Not without the inspiration of the Holy Spirit was this practice introduced into the Church." The Holy Father then goes on to warn the younger clergy especially: "Let those, therefore, among the young clergy who make light of or weaken esteem of frequent confession realize that what they are doing is foreign to the Spirit of Christ, and disastrous for the Mystical Body of our Saviour" (*Mystici Corporis Christi*, Chap. 95, Paulist ed.).

The supreme authority in the Church, then, has come on the crest of the rising tide of scholarly and devotional work which was done in the early period of the twentieth century. Without being a *laudator acti temporis* one can say that the past 50 years have seen a deeper understanding and discovery of the manifold riches of this sacrament. A more critical and discerning scholarship of the early discipline and practice of the Church has served to focus attention on the essential aspects: a sacrament in and by the Church, reconciling the sinner first to the Church and then by that very fact to God Himself. This aspect has been the main purpose of this present study. It remains only to give a brief annotated bibliographical survey of the main works in this field.

This bibliographical note is not confined to English works because most of the fundamental scholarly works remain in either French or German. Since this specific need will vary from library to library (as well as from priest to priest and layman to layman who read this bibliographical note), an asterisk has been placed before the more scholarly works which might prove too tedious and long for the average reader. The main reason for inclusion of the more scholarly works is to give librarians a general idea of what is presently being done in this field for their own bibliographical guidance. One may also consult the excellent bibliographical references in H. Rondet, *The Theology of Sin*, pp. 129–131, and B. Häring, *The Law of Christ*, V. 1, pp. 478–481.

A thorough introduction to the pastoral aspects of this problem has not been attempted in this study. Alongside the dogmatic historical and scriptural aspects of this sacrament, the psychological aspect has come to such importance that without it the priest is severely handicapped in the confessional today. No seminarian could afford to omit its study without grave spiritual harm to his ministry. For those interested in this aspect of penance, it is sufficient to recommend the magnificent and the abundant bibliography mentioned by Fathers Hagmaier and Gleason in their work, *Counselling the Catholic* (Sheed & Ward), pp. 295–302. In this respect only a few guiding works will be added.

"The doctrine of penance is complex. It presupposes a knowledge of the theology of sin and of individual sins, the theology of grace of conversion, of the virtues, in short, a knowledge of the whole of moral theology. The doctrine of penance also presupposes a knowledge of sacramental doctrine together with an understanding of psychology."[1]

1. Anciaux, P. *Le Sacrément de la Pénitence.* Louvain: Editions Nauwelaerts, 1960. (Second edition revised and augmented.)

   This is probably the best small work on the historical, pastoral, and dogmatic aspects of the sacrament of penance. In less than 260 pages, the author gives a fine résumé of early penance, ecclesiological connotations of the sacrament, and some deeply spiritual insights into its inner structure. Pastoral, dogmatic, and historical.

*2. ——— *La Théologie du Sacrément de Pénitence au XIIe Siècle.* Louvain, 1949.

   A history of the scholastic development of the diverse aspects of the sacrament of penance in the early scholastics such as Peter Abelard, William of Auvergne, Richard of St. Victor, etc., and the progressive evolution of the role of the priest and penitent, the absolution and preces, the *sacramentum, res et sacramentum,* and *sacramentum tantum.* Very telling for an understanding of penance in the West. Historical.

*3. Audet, J. P. *La Didachè: Instructions des Apôtres.* Paris: G. Gabalda, 1960.

   Although pertaining more to the realm of early Christian history, this study, however, does throw some important light on the primitive origins of the sacrament of penance. This new critical edition (reportedly one of the best) brings out some primitive implications of this sacrament in the early community. Historical.

4. Barton, John M. T. *Penance and Absolution.* New York: Hawthorn Books, 1961.

   A general exposé of the meaning of the sacrament of penance.

---

[1] A. M. Henry in *Christ in His Sacraments* (Theological Library, Vol. IV), pp. 272–273.

The argument in Scripture and early Tradition is briefly sketched and matter, form, effects, minister, etc., are briefly treated. Intended for the average layman. Popular consumption.
5. Battiffol, P. *La Iglesia Primitiva y el Catolicismo*. Buenos Aires: Ediciones Desclee de Brouwer, 1950.
   Originally a French work which is no longer available, but which appears here in Spanish translation. Interesting from the point of view of the development of the notion of penance in Origen, Tertullian, and St. Cyprian. By a master of the field of Church history. Historical.
6. Bayard, L. *Tertullien et Saint Cyprien*. Paris, 1930.
   A comparison of these two African figures in diverse doctrines. Of particular interest here is the notion of penance in these two men — the rigorist and the Catholic bishop. Historical.
7. Benevot, M., trans. *St. Cyprian: The Lapsed. The Unity of the Catholic Church*. (Ancient Christian Writers.) Westminster, Md.: Newman, 1957.
   St. Cyprian's "De Lapsis" marks a turning point in the treatment of penance as opposed to the rigorist influence in the Church. Truly Catholic in tone, it marks the beginning of a clearer concept of the sacrament for all sinners in principle of the Gospel itself. Translator's notes help explain the controversy raging at the time. Historical.
*8. Breton, V. M. *La Confession Frequent. Histoire, Valeur, Pratique*. Paris, 1945.
   One of the few works which traces frequent confession in its historical development in the West. Historical.
*9. Buchler, A. *Studies in Sin and Atonement in the Rabbinic Literature of the First Century*. London: Oxford University Press, 1928.
   Comparison and texts of Jewish notion of sin and penance during the formation of Christianity. Interesting comparison and distinction of Jewish-Christian ideas. Historical.
*10. *Canons and Decrees of the Council of Trent*, ed. by H. J. Schroeder. St. Louis: B. Herder, 1945.
   Complete texts in Latin and English translation of the 24 sessions of the Council of Trent. Of particular importance is the fourteenth session or the dogmatic definitions with regard to penance. Dogmatic.
11. Cerfaux, L. *The Church in the Theology of St. Paul*. New York: Herder & Herder, 1959.
   Valuable work on the Pauline conception of the Church. This work is indicative of the deeper understanding of the mystery of the Church which is fundamental also in understanding the sacraments as being an integration into her life

as well as in the life of God. See also along this line: Y. Congar, *The Mystery of the Church* (Baltimore: Helicon Press, 1960); H. De Lubac, *The Splendor of the Church* (New York: Sheed and Ward, 1959); F. Jurgensmeier, *The Mystical Body of Christ* (New York: Sheed and Ward, 1954); E. Mersch, *The Whole Christ* (New York: Macmillan, 1956). The value here is the relationship between the Church and the sacraments in particular. Scriptural and dogmatic.

12. Chanson, Ch. *Pour Mieux Confessor.* Arras: Brunet, 1958. (Second edition augmented.)

Excellent practical *vade mecum* for the confessor — presenting many practical cases for which the solutions are clearly and briefly presented. Rather extended as well as valuable insights on psychology, therapy, counseling, etc. Presently being translated into English. Pastoral.

13. Chery, H. C. *Frequent Confession.* London: Blackfriars, 1954.

Short devotional work on the utility (spiritual) and usefulness of frequent confession in the life of the Christian: its effects, graces, and place in Christian asceticism. Devotional.

14. *Christian Asceticism and Modern Man.* London: Blackfrairs, 1955.

Series of valuable essays on the relation of the eternal laws of penance and mortification to the modern condition of man. Approached from a physiological, psychological, historical, and scriptural point of view, the balance between penance and its accommodation to diverse modes of modern life are brought out very well. Pastoral.

15. Coates, J. R., ed. *Bible Key Words*, Vol. I. New York: Harper & Bros., 1951.

Taken from the now famous G. Kittel's *Theologisches Wörterbuch*, this particular volume contains the biblical vocabulary for sin in the Old and New Testaments. Also the biblical notion of justification included in the same volume will serve as a firm biblical foundation for a prerequisite study of penance. Biblical.

16. Community of St. Severin. *Confession.* Chicago: Fides Publishers, 1959.

General notions on the psychological and spiritual advantages of this sacrament as lived in the parish. A good attempt at integration of the dogmatic-moral into a practical working theory for laymen. Pastoral and devotional.

*17. Coppens, J. *L'Imposition des Mains et les Rites Connexes dans le N.T. et l'Eglise Ancienne.* Wettern, 1925.

A detailed (doctoral) study of the various meanings of imposition of hands as descended from the Jewish community

(Old Testament) and continued in the New. Even the sacrament of penance was conferred by such a rite. Historical.

18. *Le Coupable est il un Malade ou un Pecheur?* Paris: Spes, 1950.

This work — although now somewhat outdated — is typical of what is being accomplished in cooperation between doctors, psychologists, and moral theologians. The latter are realizing more and more that the distinctions between true guilt and false guilt, temperament, character, cnvironment, heredity, etc., all have a definite effect on the sinner. See English counterpart: Hagmaier-Gleason, *Counseling the Catholic* (New York: Sheed and Ward, 1959); W. Demal, *Pastoral Psychology in Practice* (Westminster, Md.: Newman, 1955); and many other similar works are becoming rapidly indispensable for any priest entering the confessional. Pastoral.

19. Delhaye, Ph., et al. *Théologic du Péché.* Tournai: Desclée, 1960.

Probably onc of the most exhaustive studies of the notion of sin in existence. Traces the notion of sin through Scripture, Greek philosophy, and in Catholic theology. Historical, scriptural, and dogmatic.

*20. D'Ales, A. *L'Edit de Calliste.* Paris, 1914.

A detailed historical work on the primitive origins of penance as practiced at the time of Pope Callistus who, it is claimed by the author, was the first to grant repentance to those who had committed the three "great" sins. Historical.

21. Davis, H. *Moral and Pastoral Theology,* Vol. I. New York: Sheed and Ward, 1941.

Cited only as indicative of the standard moral books covering the whole of the moral field — including the sacrament of penance. See also along these lines, J. A. McHugh and C. J. Callan, *Moral Theology, A Complete Course,* 2 vols. (New York: Wagner, 1958); Prummer, D., *Handbook of Moral Theology* (New York: Kennedy, 1958). They all repeat each other with minor deviations. Who has one, has all. Pastoral.

22. De Lubac, H. *Catholicism.* London: Burns, Oates, 1950.

Excellent essays on the sociological meaning and connotations of the seven sacraments including penance. Excellent for putting each in its ecclesial setting showing how they integrate us into God by and through the Church. Doctrinal.

*23. DeVooght, P. *La Théologie de la Pénitence.* Bruges: Beyaert, 1949.

A critical study from the scholastic fathers (mostly St. Thomas) on the inner meaning of the sacrament of penance, in relation to man, God, and the Church. Doctrinal.

24. Dirksen, A. H. *The New Testament Concept of the Metanoia.*
Washington, D. C.: Catholic University Press, 1932.
A scriptural study of the primary meaning of the Greek word
for repentance: *metanoia.* The author traces it through the
Gospels, Acts, and Epistles. Exegetical.
*25. Dondaine, H. *L'Attrition Suffisante.* Paris, 1943.
A very interesting work attempting to show the meaning of
sufficient contrition in the teaching of St. Thomas as opposed
to the Scotist and Nominalistic schools. Thomas succeeded in
integrating the two, Scotus makes an untraditional break. Historical.
*26. Doronzo, E. *Tractatus Dogmaticus de Sacramentis,* 4 vols.
Milwaukee, 1946–1956.
One of the best standard texts on the sacraments, particularly
for the sacrament of penance — attempting to show how reconciliation with the Church is *ipso facto* the *res et sacramentum*
of the sacrament of penance. Doctrinal.
27. Doyle, C. H. *Go in Peace.* New York, 1960.
Informative and readable study of the institution of the sacrament of penance. Intended for the average layman, its value
lies in the general view of this sacrament in its historical context.
Historical.
28. *L'Église et le Pecheur.* Paris: Ed. du Cerf, 1943.
Excellent series of essays on the relationship of the Church
with the sinner. Written with a pastoral intention, it deals with
the duties and meaning of the minister as well as a well-
developed chapter on the liturgy of the actual reconciliation.
Pastoral and devotional.
29. Galot, J. *La Nature du Caractère Sacrementel.* Bruges: Desclée
de Brouwer, 1956. (Museum Lessianum.)
Excellent study of the origins and development of the diverse
aspects of the sacrament characters — from the early scholastic
period to the end of the great scholastics. Its abundant bibliography makes this tool indispensable for any history of the sacrament of penance. Dogmatic.
30. Galtier, P. *Aux Origines du Sacrément de Pénitence.* Romae:
Gregorian University, 1951.
Historical development starting from pagan origins, through
the Jewish community, the New Testament, and primitive
Christianity up to the third century. One of the indispensable
works for origins. Historical.
31. ———— *L'Église et la Rémission des Péchés aux Premiers
Siècles.* Paris: Beauchesne, 1932.
One of the first historical works to deal with this matter of
the evolution of the penitential discipline — in the face of

Protestant denial of a sacrament of penance in the early Church. Historical.

32. ———— *De Poenitentia Tractatus Dogmatico-Historicus.* Rome: Gregorian University, 1950.
   A quasi condensation of elements of the above two works. Valuable text for seminary use.

33. Grotz, J. *Die Entwicklung des Busstufenevessens in der Vornicanischen Kirche.* Freiburg-im-Br., 1955.
   Historical summary of the origins and the beginnings of the sacrament of penance before the Council of Nicea (325). Historical.

34. Guardini, R. *The Conversion of Augustine.* Westminster, Md.: Newman, 1960.
   Very powerful analysis of the psychology of the sinner and his conversion as typified in the great sinner-saint, St. Augustine. Psychological.

35. Guardini, R. *Freedom, Grace and Destiny.* New York: Pantheon, 1961.
   Essays on the workings of grace in the life of modern man. The meaning of freedom and the content of action — grace in the Christian sense — elements of our existence of destiny with interesting insights in the interpretation of existence as touched by grace. Existential.

36. Guillet, J. *Themes of the Bible.* Notre Dame, Ind.: Fides, 1961.
   Very interesting biblical study of some basic notions in the Bible (sin, creation, etc.) traced through the diverse books of the Old and New Testaments. The chapter on sin as a Christian and biblical reality is very interesting from the point of view of penance. Devotional and biblical.

37. Häring, B. *The Law of Christ,* Vol. I. Westminster, Md.: Newman, 1961.
   Probably one of the most talked about works on moral theology in many years. Extremely important in emphasizing the need of making Christian charity as the very center and soul of Christian morality. In penance, the author treats of the psychology of conversion, the meaning of penance, nature and consequences of sin — both the human and divine elements. Dogmatic and pastoral.

38. Harrington, H. "The Sacrament of Penance," in *The Teachings of the Catholic Church.* New York: Macmillan, 1948.
   General exposé of the doctrine and practice of the sacrament of penance.

39. Henry, A., et al. *Pénitence et Pénitences* (Cahiers de la Roseraie). Bruges: St. André, 1953.
   Excellent series of essays on the biblical and traditional

notion of penance. Also see some fine articles on the relationship of psychology to the confessional and the excellent article on the theology of penance by the Dominican, A. Henry. Pastoral and biblical.

40. —— ed. *Christ in His Sacraments*, Theology Library, Vol. IV. Chicago: Fides, 1958, pp. 205–274.

Excellent résumé of the history and theology of this sacrament in less than 100 pages. Especially interesting is the analysis of the process of conversion in the sinner taken up biblically and psychologically. Historical and doctrinal.

*41. Heylen, V. *De Poenitentia*. Mechlinae: Dessain, 1946.

One of the better Latin texts of this tractatus. Contains some valuable pastoral insights. Its strong section is the dexterity with which the canonical problems are dealt with. Dogmatic.

42. Hildebrand, D. Von. *Transformation in Christ*. New York: Longmans, 1948.

General studies on the notion of conformity with Christ in and through the sacraments. Devotional.

43. Joret, F. D. *The Eucharist and the Confessional*. Westminster, Md.: Newman, 1955.

A comparative study of the relationship between these two sacraments and their meaning in the ecclesial context of their content. Devotional.

44. Jugemann, J. *Die Lateinischen Bussriten in Ihrer Geschichtlichen Entwicklung*. Innsbruck, 1932.

Origins of the penitential rites (inclusive of indulgences in the West). Traces them and their development from the earliest times down to the Middle Ages when they receive their quasi definitive form. Historical.

45. Kelly, G. *The Good Confessor*. Dublin, 1952.

Excellent remarks and observations on hearing confessions. Pastoral.

46. Latko, E. F. *Origen's Concept of Penance*. Quebec: University of Laval, 1949.

Interesting study of the early origins of penance and its development in Origen — one of the most important testimonies of penance in the early Church. The doctrine in the *On Leviticus*, *Against Celsus*, and the homily on Ps. 37 is here analyzed with great depth. Historical.

47. Lepicier, Cardinal H. *Indulgences, Their Origin, Nature and Development*. London: Burns, Oates, 1928.

One of the few historical studies on the beginnings of the rather historically obscure and undefined notion of indulgences as stemming from the sacrament of penance. Historical.

48. *Lumière et Vie*. Special number "Le Péché," No. 5, 1952.

Diverse essays on the biblical, historical, and psychological background for understanding what sin is in the context of Christian reality.

49. Leeming, B. *Principles of Sacramental Theology.* Westminster, Md.: Newman, 1956.

Excellent and scholarly work on the history and comparative study of diverse sacramental characters and their effects and their function in the ministry of the sacrament. Leeming accepts the opinion that reconciliation with the Church is the *res et sacramentum* of the sacrament of penance.

50. Mahoney, E. J. *Sin and Repentance.* New York: Macmillan, 1928.

A rather dated work on the meaning (Christian) of sin and repentance in the Church. Intended for the average layman, it is intended as a devotional piece.

51. Mellet, P. *La Pénitence, Sacrament d'Amitée.* Lyon, 1953.

The author proposes almost the same theory of this sacrament as does Pere Charles ("Doctrine et Pastorale du Sacrement de Penitence," in *Nouvelle Revue Théo.*, 75, May, 1953, pp. 449–40), i.e., that the sacrament of penance is the friendship reestablished principally by the absolution of the priest. True as this is — it is to be noted that not enough consideration is given to the acts of the penitent nor to penance as such, after which the sacrament is named. Theological.

52. Palmer, P., ed. *Sources of Christian Theology: Sacraments and Forgiveness.* Westminster, Md.: Newman, 1959.

Indispensable reference tool to all the principal texts from Scripture, the Fathers, and the magisterium, which refer to the sacrament of penance. Source is given fully at the end of each citation. Historical.

*53. Perinelle, A. *L'Attrition d'Après le Concile de Trente et D'Après Saint Thomas d'Aquin.* Kain, 1929.

A comparative study of the definitions of Trent and Thomistic teaching. Although exaggerating a bit on their similitude, it remains true that in general much of the definitions of Trent are strikingly similar to those of the angelic doctor. Doctrinal.

54. Pierron, J. "La Conversion, Retour à Dieu," in M. E. Boimard, et al., *Grands Themes Bibliques.* Paris, 1958, pp. 119–131.

Biblical study of the notions of penance (*metanoia*), conversion, etc., as envisioned in the biblical texts of the Old and New Testaments.

55. Pohle, J. *The Sacraments*, Vol. II, *Penance.* St. Louis: Herder, 1946.

A general doctrinal exposition of the sacrament of penance with some historical development.

56. Poschmann, B. *Die Abendlandische Kirchenbusse in Frühen Mittelalter.* Breslau, 1930.

All the books by this author are highly recommended for the most outstanding scholarship in the field of penitential research. The present volume traces the history of penance in the early Middle Ages, which is extremely important in the study of the development of private penance in the Church. Historical.

*57. ───── *Die Busse.* Freiburg-im-Br., 1951.

*58. ───── *Poenitentia Secunda.* Bonn, 1950.

Both works are indispensable tools for any detailed study of the evolution and theology of the sacrament of penance. Of particular note is the fact that Poschmann was one of the first of modern authors (along with Xiberta) to accept from his own historical studies that the reconciliation with the Church is the *res et sacramentum* of the sacrament of penance. Historical and doctrinal.

59. Regnier, J. *Le Sens du Péché.* Paris: Lethielleux, 1955.

General devotional work on the sense of sin in the Christian reality and its loss in the world of today. Interesting observations into the nature of sin for the Christian and the diverse types of sin. Pastoral and devotional.

60. Regamey, P. R. *The Cross and the Christian.* St. Louis: B. Herder Book Co., 1954.

Regamey studies the meaning of suffering and penance as positive values in the lives of Christians. He discusses the relationship of suffering and penance with regard to the Mystical Body and the plan of redemption. Devotional.

*61. Rivas, S. *La Penitencia en la Iglesia Primitiva Española.* Salamanca, 1949.

62. Rondet, H. *The Theology of Sin.* Notre Dame, Ind.: Fides, 1957.

Excellent posing of the problem in five small chapters. Rondet traces the notion of sin in early antiquity, the Old and New Testaments and finally ends with some keen pastoral insights and developments in the field of pastoral theology. Historical and pastoral.

*63. Roos, J. R. *The Seal of Confession.* Washington, D. C.: Catholic University of America Press, 1960.

Cited only as an exemplar in the canonical problems of confession. In the more than 500 works published by the canon law school of the Catholic University, libraries will find abundant canonical investigations for diverse problems. Canonical and historical.

64. Scheeben, M. J. *The Mysteries of Christianity.* St. Louis: Herder Book Co., 1958.

One of the first of the modern authors to give an ecclesial interpretation and strong emphasis on the character of the sacraments. The full development of this doctrine in function of the seven sacraments is well developed in this work. Doctrinal.

65. Schmaus, M. *Katholische Dogmatik*, B. IV, 1. Müchen, 1952, pp. 417–549.

Excellent exposé of the dogmatics of the sacrament of penance. Of particular note here is the fact that Schmaus accepts the ecclesial reconciliation theory of the *res et sacramentum* of penance. Doctrinal.

*66. Spitzig, J. A. *Sacramental Penance in the Twelfth and Thirteenth Centuries*. Washington, D. C.: Catholic University of America Press, 1948.

Traces the historical development of the form, rite, and theology of penance during these two centuries of scholastic formation. The work is definitely poor in every respect — especially in its elaboration of theology. The work of Anciaux has supplanted this book — but it might be of some value as a guide source in the English language. Historical.

67. Teetaert, A. *La Confession aux Laiques dans l'Église Latine*. Louvain, 1926.

A rather specialized work on a particular problem in the evolution of the notion of penance as a divine institution — in its contradistinction of lay ministry and clerical ministry with reference to holy orders, etc. Historical.

68. Tertullian. *Treatises on Penance: On Penitence: On Purity* (Ancient Christian Writers), trans. by W. P. LeSaint. Westminster, Md.: Newman, 1959.

Tertullian is well known for his rigorism in matters of penance (the "big three"). Here we have combined the two treatises on penance — one written as a Catholic, the other as a Montanist. The notes are very helpful in determining the vocabulary and the divergent teaching of Tertullian. Historical.

69. Thurian, Max. *Confession* (studies in ministry and worship). London: SCM Press, 1958.

Interesting work done by a Protestant in the revitalizing of many traditional aspects of the liturgy in Protestantism. We may note that although the author does not treat penance as a sacrament as such, still it is interesting to note Protestant evolution along this line. Pastoral.

70. Van Zeller, H. *Approach to Penance*. New York: Sheed and Ward, 1957.

An excellent devotional work on the meaning of penance in the spiritual life. Refreshing from the point of view of examin-

ing the subject from its essential characteristic — surrender —
than from the secondary externals. Devotional.
*71. Von Campenhausen, H. *Kirchliches Amt und Geistlichen Voll-
macht in der Ersten drei Hunderten.*
Once again, an excellent résumé of the historical origins of
the sacrament of penance. Historical.
*72. Vogel, C. *La Discipline Penitentielle en Gaule des Origines à
la fin du VII*e* Siècle.* Paris, 1952.
One of the most important works for the history of penance
not only in France but for the origins and evolution of the
forms of the sacrament in private confession as well as the
origin of the original *libri poenitentiales.* Historical.
73. Watkins, O. D. *A History of Penance.* New York: Longmans,
1920.
One of the few historical studies of this sacrament in the
English language and for that reason is indispensable in any
library treating of penance. Historical.
74. Wilson, A. *Pardon and Peace.* New York: Sheed and Ward,
1957.
Devotional and pastoral work on the meaning and application of penance into the reality of the Christian life. The
chapters on the distinction between feelings and repentance
are extremely well done. Devotional.
*75. Xiberta, B. *Clavis Ecclesiae.* Romae: Gregorian University, 1922.
The first of the modern authors to put forward the thesis that
reconciliation with the Church is the *res et sacramentum* of the
sacrament of penance. He analyzes diverse scriptural and Patristic
texts to prove his point. Violently disputed. Scriptural and
doctrinal.

Diverse Studies

1. Berdyaev, N. *Slavery and Freedom.* New York: C. Scribner,
1944.
Keen existential insights into the nature of true freedom
and slavery which comes from serving God or rejecting him
in sin or service. Psychological.
2. Carter, G. F. *Psychology and the Cross.* Milwaukee: Bruce,
1958.
This is an attempt to explain the Christian meaning of the
cross as in accord with true depth psychology and modern progress along this line. Pastoral and psychological.

3. *Conflict and Light* (studies in psychological disturbance and readjustment). New York: Sheed and Ward, 1952.

Very interesting essays on the true and false nature of guilt, and the distinction between sin, guilt, anxiety, feeling, and true repentance as contradistinguished from mental aberations. Pastoral and psychological.

4. Dobbelstein, H. *Psychiatry for Priests.* New York: J. Kenedy, 1953.

Valuable for priests who wish to start on this complicated but necessary study of at least the distinction between mental disorders and sin plus their interrelationship. Pastoral and psychological.

5. *New Problems in Medical Ethics,* ed. by D. Peter Flood, 4 vols. Westminster, Md.: Newman, 1956–1959.

Diverse problems in medical-moral difficulties and their relationship. Such problems as homosexuality, divorce, masturbation, birth control, etc., make the work invaluable. Pastoral.

6. *La Souffrance: Valeur Chretienne.* Tournai: Casterman, 1957.

The meaning of suffering and evil within the context of Christian revelation. The mystery of suffering and the gift of love is one of the profoundest chapters of the whole work. Devotional.

Index

183